Twayne's United States Authors Series

EDITOR OF THIS VOLUME

Warren French

Indiana University

Robert Penn Warren

Revised Edition

TUSAS 69

Robert Penn Warren
photo: Michael V. Carlisle

ROBERT PENN WARREN

REVISED EDITION

By CHARLES BOHNER

University of Delaware

TWAYNE PUBLISHERS
A DIVISION OF G. K. HALL & CO., BOSTON

Library of Congress Cataloging in Publication Data

Bohner, Charles H.
Robert Penn Warren.

(Twayne's United States authors series ; TUSAS 69)
Bibliography: pp. 170–72
Includes index.
1. Warren, Robert Penn, 1905–   —Criticism and interpretation.
I.   Title. II. Series.
PS3545.A748Z6 1981   813'.52   81.4269
ISBN 0-8057-7345-2   AACR2

Contents

About the Author

Charles Bohner, a native of Wilmington, Delaware, studied at Syracuse University and at the University of Pennsylvania. A member of the faculty of the University of Delaware since 1955, he has been director of the American Studies Program (1958–1968) and chairman of the Department of English (1969–1976). He has written books on two southern authors, John Pendleton Kennedy and Robert Penn Warren.

Preface to the Second Edition

The first edition of this book appeared seventeen years ago—in 1964. Although most of it had been written during 1962, I had been reading Robert Penn Warren since 1946 when *All the King's Men* appeared. Like so many of its first readers, I found that novel absorbing and believed it to be a definitive statement of the modern temper. I searched out the early novels and poetry—not an easy task, for most were out of print—and I continued to follow Warren's career as book followed book with remarkable regularity.

In reading Warren over a period which now stretches back over thirty-five years, I am aware that my interest in his career goes considerably beyond his poetry and fiction objectively considered. Warren is now a reputation and a presence, a man of letters in the old-fashioned sense of a life totally committed to literature. Each new book is a publishing event and is read and judged in the context of his entire body of work. I have reread that body of work in preparing this second edition, and I have revised some of my earlier opinions. In recording these revisions, I have the example of Warren himself, who, in revising his work for republication, has also changed his mind.

The purpose of this second edition is unchanged from that of the original study. I have tried to provide a survey of Warren's literary career, an analysis of the themes which have preoccupied him, and an account of the development of his art as it has deepened and matured. Because his writing does form, to an unusual degree, a highly unified body of work, I have taken up his writings as nearly as possible in the order in which they appeared. For despite the variety of his forms, his work has centered on several basic themes: the problem of evil, the meaning of history, and the search for self-knowledge. These themes he has returned to again and again, exploring them with a depth of perception and a richness of illustration which have placed him among the major literary figures of his time.

CHARLES BOHNER

University of Delaware

Acknowledgments

I wish to thank my wife, Jean Astolfi Bohner, who has assisted me in every stage of the preparation of this study.

I also wish to thank Mr. Robert Penn Warren and Random House, Inc., for permission to quote in this book from the following copyrighted works: *Night Rider, At Heaven's Gate, The Circus in the Attic, World Enough and Time, Brother to Dragons, Band of Angels, Segregation, Selected Essays, The Cave, The Legacy of the Civil War, Wilderness, Flood, Who Speaks for the Negro?, Homage to Theodore Dreiser, Meet Me in the Green Glen, Selected Poems: 1923–1975, Now and Then: Poems 1976–1978.*

Excerpts from Robert Penn Warren's *All the King's Men* are by kind permission of Harcourt, Brace, Jovanovich, Inc.

Chronology

1905   Robert Penn Warren born in Guthrie, Kentucky, April 24; parents, Robert Franklin and Anna Ruth Penn Warren.

1921   Graduated from Clarksville, Tennessee, high school; enrolled at Vanderbilt University.

1923–   Active in Nashville "Fugitive Group."
1925

1925   Graduated from Vanderbilt University.

1925– Graduate student at University of California (M.A., 1927).
1927

1927– Graduate student at Yale University.
1928

1928– Rhodes Scholar, Oxford (B.Litt., 1930).
1930

1929   *John Brown: The Making of a Martyr.*

1930   Assistant professor of English, Southwestern College, Memphis; married Emma Brescia.

1931– Assistant professor of English, Vanderbilt University.
1934

1934– Assistant professor of English, Louisiana State University, Baton
1942   Rouge; appointed associate professor, 1936.

1935   *Thirty-Six Poems;* founded with Charles W. Pipkin and Cleanth Brooks the *Southern Review.*

1939   *Night Rider;* Guggenheim Fellow (second fellowship awarded 1947–48).

1942   *Eleven Poems on the Same Theme;* professor of English, University of Minnesota, Minneapolis.

1943   *At Heaven's Gate.*

1944   *Selected Poems, 1923–1943;* Chair of Poetry, Library of Congress.

1946   *All the King's Men* (Pulitzer Prize).

1948   *The Circus in the Attic and Other Stories.*

1949   Motion picture of *All the King's Men;* Robert Meltzer Award, Screen Writers Guild.

1950   *World Enough and Time;* professor of playwrighting, Yale University (resigned 1956).

1951 Divorce from Emma Brescia Warren.
1952 Married Eleanor Clark; elected to American Philosophical Society.
1953 *Brother to Dragons: A Tale in Verse and Voices.*
1955 *Band of Angels.*
1957 *Promises: Poems 1954–1956* (Pulitzer Prize, National Book Award, Edna St. Vincent Millay Prize of Poetry Society of America); *Segregation: The Inner Conflict in the South.*
1958 *Selected Essays.*
1959 *The Cave;* elected to the American Academy of Arts and Letters.
1960 *You, Emperors, and Others: Poems 1957–1960; All the King's Men* (drama).
1961 *Wilderness; The Legacy of the Civil War;* professor of English, Yale University.
1964 *Flood: A Romance of Our Time.*
1965 *Who Speaks for the Negro?*
1966 *Selected Poems: New and Old 1923–1966;* Bollingen Prize in Poetry.
1968 *Incarnations: Poems 1966–1968.*
1969 *Audubon: A Vision;* National Medal for Literature; Van Wyck Brooks Award.
1970 *Selected Poems of Herman Melville: A Reader's Edition.*
1971 *Meet Me in the Green Glen; Homage to Theodore Dreiser; John Greenleaf Whittier's Poetry: An Appraisal and a Selection.*
1974 *Or Else—Poem/Poems 1968–1974;* Copernicus Prize for Poetry, Academy of American Poets; National Foundation for the Humanities Lectureship.
1975 *Democracy and Poetry;* American Academy of Arts and Sciences (received the Emerson-Thoreau Award of the academy).
1976 *Selected Poems 1923–1975.*
1977 *A Place to Come To;* Harriet Monroe Prize for Poetry.
1978 *Now and Then: Poems 1976–1978.*
1979 *Brother to Dragons: A New Version.*
1980 *Robert Penn Warren Talking: Interviews 1950–1978; Being Here.*
1981 *Jefferson Davis Gets His Citizenship Back.*

CHAPTER 1

Southern Man of Letters

R OBERT PENN WARREN was born April 24, 1905, in Guthrie, a railway junction and market town in southern Kentucky. Known locally as the Black Patch because of the dark, fire-cured tobacco grown there, the land in that section varies from gently rolling fields to scarps and rocky hillsides forested with cedar and sycamore. Pioneers from the southern uplands crossed the Alleghenies and settled there toward the close of the eighteenth century.

In this border country where sectional loyalties were often divided, Warren's family was staunchly Southern. Both his grandfathers and his granduncle fought with the Confederacy in the Civil War, and throughout his childhood he heard stories of the fighting from people who had witnessed it. His maternal grandfather, Gabriel Thomas Penn, was his chief source of information and his idol. The old veteran lived on a remote and rundown tobacco farm surrounded by his books, chiefly military history and his beloved Scott and Burns. He was indifferent to modernity and liked to say that he approved only of fly screens and painless dentistry. Impractical and bookish, he was evidently something of a trial to his daughters, but to his grandson he was the "living symbol of the wild action and romance of the past."[1] The old captain sits for his portrait in one of Warren's best poems, "Court-Martial":

> Under the cedar tree,
> He would sit, all summer, with me:
> An old man and small grandson
> Withdrawn from the heat of the day.
>
> Captain, cavalry, C.S.A.,
> An old man, now shrunken, gray
> Pointed beard clipped the classic way,
> Tendons long gone crank and wry,
> And long shrunken the cavalryman's thigh

11

Under the pale-washed blue jean. . . .
I see him now as once seen.

Warren's mother, Ruth Penn, was a schoolteacher. In his various
interviews and reminiscences, he has said little about her, perhaps in
part because he left home in 1921 at the age of sixteen and she died in
1931, about the time he was returning to Tennessee to teach. She
appears in several of his lyric elegies, most notably in the sequence
entitled "Tale of Time." She was, the speaker of the poem says, "too
precious to die."

Warren's father, Robert Franklin Warren, is described by his son in
his study of race relations, *Who Speaks for the Negro?* (1965):

He was born in 1869, son of a Confederate veteran, and raised in the Reconstruction South. His mother died when he was quite young, and his father
when he was in his teens, leaving several younger children, three of them by
a second wife who was not much older than my father himself. He buckled
down to run the family, postponing his own ambitions, studying at night,
later taking courses at a little college at night—or rather, being tutored by an
instructor at the college. I have his old Greek and German grammars, faded,
yellow, falling apart. I have lost the old copy of Dante's *Inferno* with the
illustrations by Doré, which had belonged, I think, to his father. I have the
poems he wrote; I had an anthology in which one or two were printed, more
than sixty-five years ago, but it is lost. He studied law by himself, the copies
of Blackstone and Montesquieu were in the house for years. Meanwhile he
did his duty to the family left in his charge. He got married fairly late. (99-
100)[2]

This summary is deceptively objective and low-keyed, for Warren's
relationship to his father, if we are to trust the testimony of the poetry,
was considerably more complex. Warren has returned to the subject in
several of his most ambitious and affecting poems, and the theme of
the search for the spiritual father appears obsessively in his work. "I've
been told," he says, "and I think it's true, that the 'true' and the 'false'
father are in practically every story I've written. Now what that means,
I have no idea!"[3]

I Kentucky Childhood

As a child Warren spent his winters in town attending the Guthrie
school and his summers in the country on his Grandfather Penn's farm

near Cerulean Springs, Kentucky. The summer vacations he remembers as idyllic, and on a number of occasions he has remarked on the rich store of memories and images from those days which has sustained and nurtured his art. In the fall of 1920 he entered the high school across the border in Clarksville, Tennessee, graduating at the age of fifteen.

These boyhood years were a time of economic turmoil in the Black Patch, a one-crop farming district—the entire community depended wholly on the market price of tobacco. When international tobacco trusts arbitrarily fixed prices for all classes and grades of tobacco, the local planters fought back by organizing their own associations. Attempting to force the mavericks into their fold, they formed bands of "night riders" to burn barns and scrape plant beds. The ensuing violence led to the establishment of martial law in Kentucky, and one of Warren's earliest memories concerns an encampment of state guards who had been called into Guthrie to preserve order. The melodrama of the night-rider stories was a staple of his boyhood and later provided the inspiration for his first published fiction, the novelette "Prime Leaf," and his first novel, *Night Rider* (1939).

A good deal of Warren's early education in literature was forwarded by desultory reading at home. The house was full of books, and his father would read aloud to the family, usually history and poetry. Warren had, by his own admission, no interest in writing during these years, only in reading. He shared the usual boyish admiration for "Horatius at the Bridge" and "How They Brought the Good News from Ghent to Aix." He read a "great mixture of stuff, whatever happened to come to hand—the usual nineteenth century novelists, the Boy Scout books, . . . Darwin, thrillers, detective stories." He knew intimately the King James Bible, and he has since advised young writers to read their own Bibles and mark them well. Warren also began to cultivate what would become a continuing interest in history. He read Gibbon and Macaulay, volumes on every southern shelf, and was particularly captivated by the "extraordinary romance" of American history, devouring the multi-volume works of Prescott and Parkman. But his great discovery was H. T. Buckle's *History of Civilization:*

I read Buckle and then I could explain everything. It gave me quite a hold over the other kids; they hadn't read Buckle. I had the answer to everything. Buckle was my Marx. That is, he gave you one answer to everything, and the same dead-sure certainty. After I had had my session with Buckle and the one-answer system at the age of thirteen, or whatever it was, I was somewhat inoculated against Marx and his one-answer system when he and the depression hit me and my work when I was about twenty-five. I am not being frivolous about Marx. But when I began to hear some of my friends talk about him in 1930, I thought, "Here we go again, boys." I had previously got hold of one key to the universe: Buckle. And somewhere along the way I had lost the notion that there was ever going to be just one key.[4]

Ambitious to become a naval officer, Warren applied for and received an appointment to the United States Naval Academy at Annapolis. But when an accident to his eye meant he could not pass the physical examination, he entered Vanderbilt University in the autumn of 1921, intending to study science.

II   *Vanderbilt and the Fugitives*

It was one of the remarkable strokes of good fortune in his career, as well as one of the happy coincidences of American literary history, that at that moment a number of talented people who shared an interest in writing poetry had come together in Nashville. Calling themselves the "Fugitives," the members eventually evolved one of the most influential American literary movements of the twentieth century. Discussion of the intellectual history of the South since the Civil War inevitably returns to them. Warren has called their influence upon him during his formative years "extremely important." Their magazine, the *Fugitive*, provided an outlet for his first published work, and his own subsequent career as writer, critic, and teacher has been an important force in the group's influence on American cultural life.

John Crowe Ransom, a native of Pulaski, Tennessee, and an alumnus of Vanderbilt, was the intellectual leader of the Fugitives. In 1921 Ransom, at thirty-three, had already demonstrated the gifts which would later enable him to wield vast influence on the national literary scene. In 1919 he had published a volume of verse, *Poems About God;* and during the years Warren was an undergraduate, Ransom was writing the poems which he would bring out in 1924 under the title *Chills and Fever*. Since he was a published poet, a former Rhodes scholar, and the teacher of several members of the group, Ransom naturally exerted great influence among the Fugitives. He taught Warren in freshman English and the following semester invited him to enroll in a course in advanced composition. Excited by his work under Ransom and bored by freshman chemistry, Warren discarded his plans for a scientific career and began to study literature in earnest.

During the first quarter of his sophomore year, Warren was placed in Donald Davidson's survey course in English literature. Davidson, like Ransom a native of middle Tennessee and a graduate of Vanderbilt, was another member of the Fugitives. "I first knew Robert Penn Warren," he recalled in 1958, "when he turned up in an English class I was teaching—a freckled, angular, gawky boy, yet a prodigy whom at birth the Muse had apparently vested with a complete literary equipment."[5] Davidson encouraged Warren to develop his talent for writing, excusing him from the required term papers for the course and allowing him to write imitations of Chaucer and Beowulf.

Warren spent the second and third quarters of his sophomore year studying with Walter Clyde Curry. After taking a doctorate at Stanford University, Curry had joined the Vanderbilt faculty in 1915. Although his approach to literature was philosophical and historical and his major contribution was to be in Chaucer and Shakespeare scholarship, Curry was also meeting with the Fugitives and writing poetry. Recognizing Warren's gifts, Curry lent him books, criticized his writing, and encouraged his interest in the Elizabethans, particularly John Webster and John Ford.

Their dedication to scholarship, however, had not dulled the members of the Vanderbilt English faculty to contemporary writing. When *The Waste Land* appeared in 1922, for example, it was called to Warren's attention at once by Donald Davidson, who brought him the copy of the *Dial* in which the poem appeared. And Warren had the advantage of discussing the new poetry with the young and enthusiastic faculty members under whom he was studying.

For a season poetry fever on the Vanderbilt campus was intense. "There was," Warren recalled, "just a tremendous interest in poetry among the students. There were two undergraduate writing clubs, junior and senior, where people would read poems and essays to each other. And there was an informal poetry club which met about once a week. We'd read each other's poems and booze a little, crack corn, and talk poetry. All kinds of people wrote poems then. . . . It is hard to believe now, but this is literally true: if an issue of *Dial* would come out, people would line up to get the first one. Freshmen were buying the *New Republic* or *The Nation*, to get the new poem by Yeats or the new poem by Hart Crane."[6]

The university had, of course, its limitations. It was, as Warren said

later, "a small and close provincial college." Yet the fact that the truly
gifted members of the faculty were few made their impact all the
greater. "The limitations," Warren said, "made a kind of personal
focus on individuals and on ideas; I remember this quite distinctly,
since some of these people represented the great world of ideas and
the great world of geography, of wider horizons, in a very special way
which is no longer true in educational institutions."[7]

Equally significant for Warren's personal literary development during these years was the friendship of another undergraduate and fellow
Kentuckian, Allen Tate. Tate was twenty-one years old and entering
upon his senior year in the fall of 1921 when Warren came to Vanderbilt. That year Tate had accepted an invitation from Davidson to
join the Fugitives, for he had fallen under the spell of both Davidson
and Ransom. "At that early age," he said, they "meant just about
everything." Tate brought to the group the boldness of youth, a taste
for the *avant-garde* in literature, and a total commitment to poetry.
For Tate, Warren said, it was "poetry or death."

Tate has written an amusing account of his first meeting with Warren. During the spring of 1923, Tate, busily typing a poem in the bach-
elor quarters of Walter Clyde Curry, saw a young man wander into
the room, "the most remarkable looking boy" he had ever seen:

> He was tall and thin, and when he walked across the room he made a
> sliding shuffle, as if his bones didn't belong to one another. He had a long
> quivering nose, large brown eyes, and a long chin—all topped by curly red
> hair. He spoke in a soft whisper, asking to see my poem; then he showed me
> one of his own—it was about Hell, and I remember this line:
>
> > Where lightly bloom the purple lilies . . .
>
> He said he was sixteen years old and a sophomore. This remarkable young
> man was "Red," Robert Penn Warren, the most gifted person I have ever
> known.[8]

Tate, impressed by Warren's early attempts at writing poetry,
insisted that he show them to the editors of the *Fugitive* and of the
Double Dealer, a little magazine which had begun publishing in New
Orleans in 1920. As a result, Warren soon had the satisfaction of seeing
his work appear in both magazines. Led through his interest in Bau-
delaire and the French Symbolists to a close acquaintance with the
work of Ezra Pound and T. S. Eliot, Tate communicated his enthusi-

asm for these writers to Warren. Tate's considerable influence on the younger Warren led several of the Fugitives to consider him a follower. "I am content for the moment at least," Warren wrote Tate, "and you should be happy for a bright disciple." For his part, Tate never doubted Warren's genius. Speaking of some verses Warren had written for the book page of the *Nashville Tennessean,* Tate wrote Davidson: "That boy's a wonder—has more sheer genius than any of us; watch him: his work from now on will have what none of us can achieve—power."[9]

Tate introduced Warren to another member of the Fugitives, Ridley Wills. Wills's undergraduate career had been interrupted by army service in World War I, and he had returned to the campus glowing with the prestige of a first novel entitled *Hoax.* He was, in Tate's opinion, "small, graceful, ebullient, and arrogant, and one of the wittiest and most amusing [of] companions." The three friends determined to room together in Wesley Hall, a dormitory for theological students, and no place, Tate said, "for the Heathen." This period in their lives, as described by Tate, was wildly exciting, a mixture of undergraduate prankishness and serious intellectual discussion:

> In order to get into bed at night we had to shovel the books, trousers, shoes, hats and fruit jars onto the floor, and in the morning, to make walking-space, we heaped it all back upon the beds. We stuck pins into Red while he slept to make him wake up and tell us his dreams. Red had made some good black-and-white drawings in the Beardsley style. One day he applied art gum to the dingy plaster and when we came back we saw four murals, all scenes from *The Waste Land.* I remember particularly the rat creeping softly through the vegetation, and the typist putting a record on the gramophone.[10]

Wills and Tate began taking Warren to Fugitive meetings while he was still a sophomore, although he was not made a member of the group until the spring of his junior year. The meetings, held informally at the home of one of the members, were a revelation to the shy and impressionable Warren. The group was in earnest about the significance of poetry as a serious undertaking. "I got the feeling," Warren recalled, "that poetry was a vital activity, that it related to ideas and to life." From the first, the discussions put great emphasis on a rigorous and searching attention to the structure of poetry. The author would read his composition aloud, while the members of the group followed the text from typed copies which had been prepared for them. Perhaps the reading might be followed by comments of a general nature or by a murmur of compliments, but more likely it was greeted by a ruminative silence. The discussion that followed was, by custom and agreement, skeptical and frank. The poem was subjected to an exhaustive and probing analysis, and any weakness in rhyme, rhythm, or imagery was ruthlessly exposed. The merely facile or conventional exercise in verse was likely to be dismissed without much comment. This habit of formalistic, intensive criticism undoubtedly shaped the habits of composition of the group and carried over into their private conversations concerning their work. John Crowe Ransom employed a similar technique in his advanced writing courses, stressing theories of prosody and scrutinizing in detail selected poems from English literature. And this method of close textual analysis, broadened and systematized, provided the method of Warren's *Understanding Poetry* (1938), written in collaboration with Cleanth Brooks, a work which profoundly altered the teaching of poetry in college classrooms.

For Warren, association with the Fugitives not only offered a stimulus and a discipline but also provided an outlet for publication. During his junior and senior years, he published twenty-four of his poems in the *Fugitive*, and in his last year at Vanderbilt he was asked to assume some of the editorial responsibilities. While grateful for the opportunities that association with the group afforded, Warren seems not to have been entirely sympathetic with the Fugitives and their methods. In the spring of 1924 he wrote to Tate: "I value your criticism a good deal more than any other I receive, for you know the sort that comes out in a Fugitive meeting."

In 1956 Warren, in looking back on the Fugitive years, was amazed that the fellowship should have seemed to others a unified movement. "A few years after I left Vanderbilt, people began to refer to those people [the Fugitives] as a unit, as if there were a church or an orthodoxy. I was so shocked by that . . . because I was so aware of the differences of temperament, and the differences of opinions . . . but the notion of a unity had just never occurred to me, except that the unity was just purely a unity of friendship and common background." [11]

III   *John Brown*

Upon graduating *summa cum laude* from Vanderbilt in 1925, Warren entered the University of California at Berkeley to undertake graduate study in English. If he had found cause for discontent with the

Fugitives during his last year at Vanderbilt, it was soon dissipated in the atmosphere of Berkeley. He thought the literary men there "fifty years behind the times." At Nashville the talk had been all Pound and Eliot, but at Berkeley the campus intellectuals discoursed interminably about Marx and Engels. Warren nevertheless settled into the routine of graduate work and in 1927 received the Master of Arts degree. He was now firmly committed to advanced study in English literature, and in the fall of 1927 he entered Yale for additional work. He was, he said, "following scholarships. Whenever I got a scholarship, the biggest scholarship, that's where I went."[12]

During the summer of 1928, Warren was in New York visiting Allen Tate, who, with his wife Caroline Gordon, was moving in the literary circle which included Scott Fitzgerald, Hart Crane, Edmund Wilson, and John Peale Bishop. Attempting to establish himself by free-lance writing, Tate had brought out a biography of Stonewall Jackson in the late spring of 1928 and was hard at work on a life of Jefferson Davis which appeared in November 1929. Through Tate's acquaintanceship with the literary agent Mavis McIntosh, Warren secured a commission from the recently established firm of Payson and Clarke to write a biography of John Brown. Warren plunged into the task with enthusiasm, making the trip to Harpers Ferry to interview the last surviving witness of John Brown's raid. *John Brown: The Making of a Martyr*, published in November 1929, received a handful of good reviews, but it sold few copies in that disastrous season of the Great Crash.

Warren's life of John Brown is a substantial achievement. Considered as the first book of a young man of twenty-four and as one written while he was simultaneously engaged in graduate study, it is an astonishing demonstration of his precocity and his creative energy. The biography reveals how early Warren's special gifts matured: his ability to render a scene palpably and memorably, and his skill at wringing from a story every ounce of color and drama. Earlier biographies of Brown had tended to be written by either the prosecuting attorney or the counsel for the defense. Although Warren is clearly not in sympathy with his protagonist, he is obviously trying to be scrupulously fair in his weighing of evidence. Such weaknesses as the book possesses are those of the neophyte scholar. Warren has a tendency to lose sight of his hero in his zeal to untangle the skein of political history. He occasionally succumbs to the temptation to linger over a disputed point in the evidence at the cost of the movement of his narrative. And his balanced handling of his materials is sometimes marred by an obtrusive tone of youthful flippancy and heavy irony. The book is, he said later, "shot through with Southern defensiveness, and in my ignorance the psychological picture of the hero was presented far too schematically."[13]

As Warren interprets his career, Brown is a man laboring under a "profound compulsion," possessed by an idea and enamored of violence. Like his Puritan forebears, John Brown fancies himself one of the elect; and like those rarified descendants of the Puritans, the Transcendentalists, he surrenders himself to an idea without regard for its practical consequences in an imperfect world. Brown, in Warren's view, is a man blissfully untroubled by self-knowledge. In his stiff-necked insistence on being in the right, he represents a type which has fascinated Warren ever since: the man who possesses or develops an "elaborate psychological mechanism for justification" (446). Brown finds his justification in a single abstraction—freedom. "The word 'Freedom' obscured every selfish motive, and transformed . . . every act of criminality or violence into something worthy and excellent" (264). Sustained by his egotism, Brown was guilty of a "fundamental error." He "thought of slavery in terms of abstract morality, and never in the more human terms of its practical working" (331). Other giants of the era, in Warren's opinion, were seduced by the same tendency toward abstraction: the young Lincoln, for example, "the shambling, awkward Cassandra of Illinois," and Ralph Waldo Emerson, "a man who lived in words, big words, and not in facts." Finally, John Brown, donning the mantle of an Old Testament prophet, is a man who confounds means with ends:

> [John Brown's] own will and God's will were one. Hypocrisy is too easy a word to use here, and too simple. If John Brown had no scruple at deception it was because the end justified the means. That end, that goal, which beckoned year after year, seemed to float and shift and change its shape like some mirage. In other words, John Brown's enormous egotism expressed itself in one set of terms after another, and after Harper's Ferry there would be a final transposition of this egotism into new terms. In his past history these terms had become larger, more impersonal, more dignified, and justification under them had become easier. . . . Does man's will need justification beyond the will of God? (351)

John Brown is a modest contribution to American history, valuable and instructive in its own right. But for the student of Warren's career, it is chiefly interesting in the way it presages the characteristic preoccupations of his later work. The biography was, as Warren said later, a "step toward fiction."[14] The John Brown who emerges from Warren's pages is the spiritual ancestor of a number of the heroes of Warren's novels, and the biography adumbrates a number of the themes that he has returned to again and again. The man who single-mindedly follows an idea to a violent end, the man doomed by his lack of self-knowledge, the man caught in the dilemma of reconciling evil means with a desirable end—these form the thematic matrix of Warren's fiction.

IV   *Rhodes Scholar*

When the biography of Brown appeared in 1929, Warren was at Oxford, where he had gone in the fall of 1928 as Rhodes scholar from Kentucky. He had accepted the award with the knowledge that he was following in the footsteps of his teacher and fellow Fugitive at Vanderbilt, John Crowe Ransom, who had been at Christ Church College from 1910 to 1913. Another Fugitive, William Y. Elliott, later professor of government at Harvard, had been at Balliol College from 1921 to 1923. Elliott had served for a year as an English instructor at Vanderbilt and, together with Allen Tate, had introduced Warren to some of the new poetry. Warren was joined at Oxford by another Vanderbilt alumnus and Rhodes scholar, Cleanth Brooks—the two friends there laying the groundwork for their lifelong collaboration.

It was an exciting time to be living abroad, but the experience brought Warren a sense of detachment concerning his life in Kentucky and Tennessee and a sense of nostalgia as well—"the look back home from a long distance." In the spring of 1930 Warren received a letter from Paul Rosenfeld, who, with Van Wyck Brooks and Lewis Mumford, was editing the *American Caravan*, inviting him to submit a long story. Rosenfeld had heard Warren reminiscing about his boyhood memories of the night riders in Kentucky and had suggested that the stories would make excellent material for fiction.[15] As a result, Warren stole time from his academic work at Oxford to write "Prime Leaf," a novelette which Rosenfeld accepted and which appeared in the *American Caravan* for 1931.

"Prime Leaf" deals with the impact on a small boy of a quarrel between his grandfather and father over the terroristic tactics of an association of tobacco growers who have organized a band of "night riders" to resist a monopoly of eastern buyers. The father's involvement in the scheme leads him to shoot one of the night riders and ultimately

to be ambushed and murdered himself. The story is a polished performance which abounds with intensely realized scenes of the tobacco
farms and small towns of Warren's youth. The narrative power which
he had already displayed in his biography of John Brown is enhanced
in the story by a talent for dialogue, a keen ear for the nuances of
dialect and the rhythms of human speech. The reader finds, in embryo,
themes that would continue to concern Warren: the ways of violence,
the adaptation of means to ends, and the mixture of love, jealousy, and
guilt in the relation of father and son. But Warren had not by any
means exhausted the reservoirs of memory, for a decade later the
themes only dimly shadowed forth in "Prime Leaf" were developed
on a larger scale in his first novel, *Night Rider.*

During his temporary expatriation in England, Warren did not lose
touch with the Fugitives in Nashville. Although their magazine expired
in December 1925, the leading spirits of the group, Ransom and Davidson, were teaching at Vanderbilt; and Tate, although living in New
York, kept in close touch through correspondence. Louise Cowan, in
her study of the Fugitives, has shown that in the late 1920s they were
becoming concerned over the course the South was charting in public
affairs. During the early years of the decade, their interests had centered on poetry and philosophy, and insofar as they were conscious of
being southerners, they were intent on repudiating the magnolia-and-
julep tradition of southern letters. As the forward to the first issue of
the *Fugitive* put it: "*The Fugitive* flees from nothing faster than from
the high-caste Brahmin of the Old South." The contributors to the
magazine would have condemned sectional identity as a provincial
hindrance to their own development as artists and as men.

But as industrialism made greater inroads into the South after World
War I, some of the Fugitives were growing increasingly dissatisfied
with the direction the region was taking. In 1925 the notorious Scopes
"Monkey Trial" in Dayton, Tennessee, had fostered the image of a
bigoted and antiintellectual South. Attacks in the northern press, of
which H. L. Mencken's "The Sahara of the Bozart" is the most famous,
were baiting the South and its traditional ways. The Fugitives were
distressed by what they considered to be the results of a culture based
on the machine: the accelerating tempo of life, the chaotic individu-
alism, the blatant materialism, the debasement of human effort and
human dignity. The artist in such a society was particularly vulnerable,
for the pressures of mass culture were corrupting taste and commer-
cializing art.

It was just at this point that the history of the South offered a parable applicable to modern America. The South, even in defeat, had resisted the siren song of the machine and had clung doggedly to its agricultural ways. If, when judged against the Yankee Cult of Success, southern society seemed slow and backward, it nevertheless cherished the values of family tradition and grace of manner and nurtured the esthetic and spiritual impulse. The so-called "New South," in its haste to share in the material fruits of industrial progress, was selling its birthright. The capitulation to northern industrialism was particularly stultifying to the artist. As Donald Davidson said: "The Southern tradition in which these writers would share has been discredited and made artistically inaccessible. . . . One has to look closely at the provincial Southern artists to discover traces of the indigenous Southern."[16]

V   The Agrarian Movement

In 1930 after much discussion and debate, four of the Fugitives—Ransom, Davidson, Tate, and Warren—joined eight other southerners in writing *I'll Take My Stand* (1930), a collection of essays in support of a southern way of life "against what may be called the American or prevailing way." All twelve southerners subscribed to a prefatory "Statement of Principles," a catalogue of the ills of industrialism written by Ransom and crystallizing the distinction between the two ways of life in the phrase "Agrarian *versus* Industrial." From Oxford, Warren sent an essay entitled "The Briar Patch," a discussion of the race question and a defense of segregation.

Characteristically, Warren treats the subject historically, briefly tracing the stages by which the South—and the North—reached the present dilemma. The panacea he offers is gradualism, the mutual and patient education of both Negroes and whites; for the problem of the poor and illiterate Negro is inextricable from the problem of the poor and illiterate white. Warren aligns himself with the general economic and political tenor of *I'll Take My Stand* by pointing out that the tendency of industrialism to intensify competition and to uproot the Negro from his traditional and accustomed role on the farm will exacerbate the situation. The argument, however, is not without its contradiction. Warren has faith in education, but he knows that good education is expensive and that the South is poor. Consequently, "the increasing prosperity of the section may give considerable hope for the future." The northern reader, smarting under the attack on his system, would be quick to note that such prosperity as the South enjoys is that based on the despised industrialism. Fundamentally, however, Warren sees the problem as a moral one: "What the white workman must learn, and his education may be as long and laborious as the negro's, is that he may respect himself as a white man, but, if he fails to concede the negro equal protection, he does not properly respect himself as a man" (260).

As a result of Warren's shortlived connection with the Agrarians, he has been repeatedly associated with a socioeconomic thesis which his later work in part repudiates and ultimately transcends. While in sympathy with the broad humanistic aims of the contributors to *I'll Take My Stand,* he doubted the wisdom of the title and wished to call the book *Tracts Against Communism.* Nor, in retrospect, did he feel satisfied with his treatment of the race problem. "I remember," he said later, "the jangle and wrangle of writing the essay and some kind of discomfort in it, some sense of evasion." As for his argument, the need for the establishment of "an informed and productive negro community," the forces for social justice unleashed since World War II have rendered it obsolete. As a temporary expedient for its time, it was sensible enough. As Warren said, "There wasn't a power under heaven that could have changed segregation in 1929—the South wasn't ready for it, the North wasn't ready for it, the Negro wasn't."[17] Personally, Warren has completely reversed his earlier position. After pondering the problem for a number of years, Warren undertook a trip in 1956 through the section of the South he had known best—Kentucky, Tennessee, Arkansas, Mississippi, and Louisiana—the result of which was his long essay *Segregation: The Inner Conflict in the South.*

This book is a superb piece of journalism, a report of conversations the author had with southerners and with himself. It is an eminently temperate and wise consideration of the race situation in the South. Without editorializing and without rancor, Warren dramatically builds up, in a wide-ranging dialogue between black and white, a picture of the daily humiliations that segregation imposes on both the oppressor and the oppressed. In contrast to his treatment of the question in "The Briar Patch," Warren clearly sounds the moral imperative. Segregation is not, however, a question of abstract morality; "it has to be solved in a context for possible solutions" (113). And the essential problem is not "to learn to live with the Negro. It is to learn to live with ourselves" (111). If nothing else, *Segregation* reveals the complex domestic implications of the race question in the South. At the heart of the matter is

the pervasive and paradoxical sense of community. Warren, probing
the motives for segregation, crystallizes this sense of community in two
brief conversations:

> Pridefulness, money, level of intelligence, race, God's will, filth and dis-
> ease, power, hate, contempt, legality—perhaps these are not all the words
> that get mentioned. There is another thing, whatever the word for it. An
> eminent Negro scholar is, I suppose, saying something about the other thing.
> "One thing," he says, "is that a lot of people down here just don't like change.
> It's not merely desegregation they're against so much, it's just the fact of any
> change. They feel some emotional tie to the way things are. A change is
> disorienting, especially if you're pretty disoriented already." . . . And I hear
> a college student in the Deep South: "You know, it's just that people don't
> like to feel they're spitting on their grandfather's grave. They feel some con-
> nection they don't want to break. Something would bother them if they broke
> it."
> The young man is, I gather, an integrationist. He adds: "And sometimes
> something bothers them if they don't break it."
> Let us give a name now to whatever it is that the eminent Negro scholar
> and the young white college boy were talking about. Let us, without meaning
> to be ironical, call it piety. (55–56)

Warren understands this paradox at the center of southern life, this
powerful sense of history that at once vitalizes and vitiates life in the
South. It is a constant tension in his own writing, and it is his awareness
of its significance that drew him into the camp of the Agrarians. In
1956 the Fugitives reassembled at Vanderbilt University for a reunion.
The talk turned to a consideration of the Agrarian movement and its
ultimate meaning both for the United States and for the men who
sponsored it. "For me," Warren said, "it was a protest . . . against a
kind of de-humanizing and disintegrative effect on your notion of what
an individual person could be. . . . The past is always a rebuke to the
present. . . . It's a better rebuke than any dream of the future. It's a
better rebuke because you can see what some of the costs were, what
frail virtues were achieved in the past by frail men."[18]

But no matter how troubled the South might have been, Warren
chose to return there when, in 1930, he came back from Oxford to
begin his career as a teacher of English. Yale had offered him a fellowship to complete his doctorate in Elizabethan literature. But at the last
minute he turned it down and, as if to seal his commitment to writing,
took a vow never to contribute an article to a professional journal.[19] He

spent a year at Southwestern College in Memphis, moving on the following year to his alma mater, Vanderbilt. At the end of three years Vanderbilt did not renew his contract, and in 1934 he joined the English department at Louisiana State University, just as the flamboyant Huey Long, then at the height of his power, was lavishing money and attention on the university.

Much has been written of the dangers of academe to the creative writer. Warren himself has dissected the stifling atmosphere of the small college in two short stories. "The Life and Work of Professor Roy Millan" is a scathing study of a man whose soul has been withered by the niggling economies and pathetic self-deceptions that compose life in a small, rural college. Similarly, the central character in "The Unvexed Isles," Professor Dalrymple, has found the role of college teacher an escape upward from a boyhood of dirt farms and poverty into the rigid hierarchy of southern gentility. Both stories are primarily studies in atmosphere, evoking the pallid and pretentious community of the rural college, tense with the strain of preserving appearances and vitiated by small vanities and petty jealousies.

However, Warren's own career and his comments on the teaching profession contradict the testimony of his fiction. In 1939, after a decade of academic life, he concluded that in general it was helpful: "For a person who wants to write, the advantages of teaching, I believe, outweigh the disadvantages; a teacher is forced to clarify—or to try to clarify—his own mind on certain questions which are necessarily involved in the business of writing."[20] A decade later his opinion was unchanged: "There are very fundamental compensations in teaching if you're in the right kind of place and have the right kind of students. . . . A university has the failures and defects of institutions, just like government or the family or anything else. But I do think it gives certain perspectives in its better reaches that you'd not get if you were outside."[21]

VI   The Southern Review

During Warren's years at Lousiana State University, he founded with Cleanth Brooks and another Vanderbilt alumnus, Charles W. Pipkin, the *Southern Review*, which quickly became one of the foremost literary and critical quarterlies in the nation. The tables of contents glitter with illustrious names: W. H. Auden, Kenneth Burke, T. S. Eliot, Ford Madox Ford, Aldous Huxley, Katherine Anne Porter, John Crowe

Ransom, Wallace Stevens, and Allen Tate. The editors had a gift for spotting new talent as well, and the *Southern Review* sponsored the early work of such writers as Nelson Algren, R. P. Blackmur, Randall Jarrell, Mary McCarthy, F. O. Matthiessen, Delmore Schwartz, and Eudora Welty.

The purpose of the magazine was to contribute to the cultural life of the South and the editors, naturally enough, hoped it would become the focal point of that life. The title itself was an expression, as they said, "of the regional and sectional piety of the editors."[22] There was, however, a conscious desire to avoid any taint of provincialism or chauvinism. No attempt was made to limit the contributions to those from the South or to insist on local color in subject matter or regional consciousness in treatment. Eventually the magazine had a list of contributors and a circulation that belied any charge of parochialism. It reached a circulation of approximately fifteen hundred, and, as the editors observed, their lists included more readers in Calcutta and Tokyo than in Atlanta, Georgia.

In 1942 the publication was suspended by order of the president of the university. There were a number of reasons for its demise. Several members of the faculty were hostile, and certain officers of the administration felt that, during wartime, the journal was a luxury the university could not afford. Others had been critical of the magazine as unrealistic and remote from the fundamental concerns of a university. With the suspension of the magazine, Warren left Louisiana State to take a position as professor of English and director of the creative writing program at the University of Minnesota.

Warren's appointment to the new post calls attention to another concern, in fact the central concern, which had occupied him while teaching in the South. Throughout these years, as he said, "my deep and abiding desire was to write poetry and fiction, and even though I felt no competition between this desire and the profession I enjoyed, I turned most of my energy, when I left the classroom and the obligations of the classroom, toward writing poems and stories and novels."[23] Warren had published a number of short stories during the 1930s, and he had in progress a novel dealing with the world of his Kentucky boyhood. But because the writing of verse had been his absorbing interest since Fugitive days, it is to a consideration of the achievement of his early poetry that we must first turn.

CHAPTER 2

The Texture of the World

IN THE spring of 1943 Robert Penn Warren published in the *Kenyon Review* an essay entitled "Pure and Impure Poetry" which has since taken its place among the major texts of modern criticism. Warren himself evidently believed the essay constituted an important personal statement, for he subsequently placed it first in his *Selected Essays* (1958). Since the essay appeared while he was preparing his *Selected Poems, 1923–1943* for the press, he was perhaps prompted to speculate on the nature of poetry by looking back on two decades of his own practice of the art.

I *Poetic Beginnings*

"Poetry," Warren begins, "wants to be pure but poems do not." The poet writing the pure poem is, like the laboratory scientist, working under carefully controlled conditions to extract the emotion pure and undefiled. The pure poem is the distillate, the emotion purged of the dross of ambiguity. Warren insists, however, that the poem must have its being not in the aseptic laboratory but in the world. Consequently, the poem must, like life itself, partake of impurities: "cacophonies, jagged rhythms, ugly words and ugly thoughts, colloquialisms, clichés, sterile technical terms, headwork, and argument, self-contradictions, clevernesses, irony, realism—all things which call us back to the world of prose and imperfection." If, for example, the pure poet (Warren's examples are Shelley and Tennyson) treats of love, he is likely to represent it as ethereal and beautiful and pure. Love is for him a "soft" subject, and he will insist on its "softness." But, Warren argues, it is just this insistence which leads to the downfall of the pure poet. Love may be bawdy and sensual and comic. If the poem does not contain some awareness of this paradoxical nature of love, some ironic counterstatement, the poem is vulnerable to parody and ridicule. The result may be an "embarrassing" poem or a "naked" poem. Warren's ideal poet "is like the jujitsu expert; he wins by utilizing the resistance of his opponent—the materials of the poem. In other words, a poem, to be good, must earn itself."

In terms of his own definition, Warren's poetry is decidedly impure. From his first verses, written while still an undergraduate at Vanderbilt, he has readily introduced into his poetry all of the elements so troubling to the pure poet. Warren employs, for example, a remarkable variety of metrical forms, often in startling combinations. Sudden contrasts between elegance and earthiness abound in his verse—the coupling of a Latinic adjective and an Anglo-Saxon noun and the mixing of esoteric diction with slang. The folk speech of his native Kentucky and Tennessee is a Warren hallmark, his ear for dialect going beyond mere quirks of vocabulary or oddities of syntax. In its system of tensions, his poetry harks back to the elaborately fashioned and intellectually rigorous verse of the decidedly impure Metaphysicals. The result is a poetry of tartness and astringency which lays him open to the charge that has been made against his former teacher and fellow Fugitive, John Crowe Ransom, a deficiency in verbal music.

Warren was undoubtedly influenced by Ransom, as was an entire generation of Southern poets. Ransom's students include Allen Tate, Randall Jarrell, and Robert Lowell. "Perhaps," Robert Lowell said, "their being with Ransom was an irrelevant accident. And yet, I think the teacher may have made the difference."[1] In "Pure and Impure Poetry" Warren pays high tribute to Ransom by including at the center of the essay an admiring explication of the metrical brilliance and ironic wit of "Bells for John Whiteside's Daughter." Ransom, on his part, called Warren "one of the really superlative poets of our time."[2]

During the two years he was associated with the Fugitives, Warren published more than a score of poems in their magazine. "Crusade," his first poem to be accepted for publication, appeared in the number for June 1923, and in February 1924 his name was added to the masthead of the magazine. While his poems do not appear to disadvantage beside the work others were contributing, Warren's verses are not remarkably superior to those of many talented young people whose interest in literature stimulates them to write poetry. Generally traditional in form, these early poems are characterized by a fascination with the macabre and the monstrous. Warren's imagination seems to have been haunted by images of putrefaction and disease. Death is everywhere, generally at its most hideous—"naked corpses," "skulls glaring white," "flies on bloated bodies," in a world of "leprous" mists, "shriveling" ferns, and "obscene" wheat. The tone is melodramatic, a turgid and overwrought straining for effect. Only when Warren turns to material he knows intimately, notably in the lyric elegy "Alf Burt, Tenant Farmer," do we catch glimpses of real promise.

During the spring of 1924, Warren, then nineteen years old, sank into a depression and apparently tried to take his own life. Allen Tate wrote to Donald Davidson: "Don't deceive yourself that he did it because he was 'convinced he would never be a poet.' It shows, finally,—that statement—his fundamental courage. He rejected the meaner way, that of telling the truth about his anguish. Red is no simpleton; it isn't a mere despair of youth, a maudlin self-pity working itself into the hysteria of suicide. It is simply that he has been beaten down so consistently and brutally, that his emotional needs have met frustration so completely, that he was driven into a blind alley."[3]

Warren recovered his health and graduated from Vanderbilt in 1925. He spent the summer revising and polishing his early poems for publication. He told Allen Tate that he had about thirty-eight in his portfolio, but that he had "few illusions about them." And he wrote to Andrew Lytle in August 1925, "I think that my philosophy of poetry is right, at least for me, who am a relativist and who consequently would not erect it into a criterion. I feel that it is right, but I also know that my method demands discipline; it is far too romantic in essence with too much sarcasm. I have never achieved a real irony which is the true alloy."[4]

II   Thirty-Six Poems

Ultimately he determined against publication, and another decade was to pass before he brought out in 1935 his first volume of verse under the title *Thirty-Six Poems*. In preparing the volume for the press, Warren winnowed out much of his early work. The only poem that survives from undergraduate days is "To a Face in a Crowd," which had appeared in the *Fugitive* (June 1925) and was later included in *Fugitives: An Anthology of Verse* (1928). The poem, clearly the best of his earlier work, is representative of it in tone and theme. The form is traditional four-line, iambic pentameter stanzas; the mood is Eliotic. As the title suggests, the poem is a plea for communion with a stranger whose "face is blown, an apparition, past." The setting is a place of "bitter waters" where "among the rocks the faint lascivious grass / Fingers in lust the arrogant bones of men." The speaker feels that he has seen the face before, perhaps in a dream. He can address the stranger as "my brother," for together they share a dark and violent history which they have no choice but to confront. The speaker knows, too, that such tenuous communion as is possible between them must be based on a recognition of their common past.

> . . . we must meet
> As weary nomads in this desert at last,
> Borne in the lost procession of these feet.

The rest of *Thirty-Six Poems* shows great strides beyond such early work. In his essay on Robert Frost, Warren has defined the poet as "the man who is greatly concerned with the flux of things, with the texture of the world, with, even, the dark 'natural' places of man's soul."[5] So it is with Warren's own poems. His work confronts the elemental facts of human experience, and yet, as might be expected, it is deeply rooted in his native region. "The Last Metaphor" and "Croesus in Autumn," for example, offer frequent glimpses of Kentucky landscape, vivid with precisely observed and sharply focused images. This deeply felt sense of place never descends into mere local color but is the wellspring of the poetry's vitality. The predominant mood is autumnal: falling leaves, the sound of wind in barren boughs, "the scent of the year's declension." The poetry is suffused with a sense of natural forces at work—the cycle of the seasons, the generations of men, the flow of time.

A case in point is the series of lyrics written between 1927 and 1932 and grouped under the title "Kentucky Mountain Farm." In the opening "Rebuke of the Rocks," the rocks address the "little stubborn people of the hill," instructing them that the "little flesh and fevered bone / May keep the sweet sterility of stone." But even the rocks are at the mercy of massive natural processes, for

> the frost has torn
> Away their ridgéd fundaments at last,
> So that the fractured atoms now are borne
> Down shifting waters to the tall, profound
> Shadow of the absolute deeps. . . .

In "History Among the Rocks" the speaker wonders about the young soldiers, "grey coats, blue coats," slaughtered on the very mountainside where the farm now stands. He reflects on the ways a man may die: freezing in winter snow, drowning in a spring flood, poisoning by a copperhead while harvesting summer wheat. The violence inherent in each way of dying is muted by the poet's treatment. Freezing to death is but "a cold and crystalline dream"; the drowned man is "hushed in the end" as the waters "gently bend." Considered against the cycle of the year, such deaths are but the course of nature, the inevitable risks of life. By contrast, "Young men on the mountainside / Clambered, fought. Heels muddied the rocky spring." The men sought death in "these autumn orchards." They fought furiously, died violently, and their deaths seem somehow to violate the natural order. The speaker is puzzled by their motives:

> Their reason is hard to guess, remembering
> Blood on their black mustaches in moonlight.
> Their reason is hard to guess and a long time past:
> The apple falls, falling in the quiet night.

The ending is a characteristic Warren signature. The final image is cryptic, at most an oblique suggestion of the meaning of the experience described in the poem. Compared to the men killed by natural calamities, the soldiers have consciously chosen to court death. Perhaps it is the exercise of this choice that lends dignity and meaning to their lives. The poet does not say; he merely points to the fall of the apple, an image suggesting the vast natural forces at work in the universe against which the soldiers' decision must be measured.

Among these early poems we find the first tentative exploration of themes and techniques which Warren returns to and develops in his later poetry and fiction. "Letter of a Mother" and "The Return: An Elegy" are preliminary sketches for one of the most familiar narrative patterns of Warren's later work. Each dramatizes, by a cycle of flight and return, the mingled feelings of love, responsibility, and guilt between a mother and her son. The son, driven by a dimly felt need for self-realization, flees the family homestead only to be haunted by a nagging sense of filial obligation.

In "The Return," the best of Warren's early work, we hear the first confident sounding of his characteristic poetic voice. The elegy develops by a series of violent shifts in tone. The speaker is hurrying westward to the bedside of his dying mother. In the darkness the pines whip past the Pullman window, stimulating in the son's mind a chain of grotesque and irreverent associations. The glimpses of Southern landscape, swept by rain squalls and low-hanging mists, merge with childhood memories, speculations on the pioneers who first made the journey westward, and sudden and uncontrollable spasms of guilt ("the old bitch is dead / what have I said!"). The speaker imagines, or remembers, a dead fox lying amidst ferns and blossoms, and his imagination clothes the scene in the formal trappings of a funeral ("the gracious catafalque and pall"). His mind irrationally metamorphoses the memory of the fox into the memory of his mother ("the old fox is dead / what have I said"). Images rise in the mind, combine and recombine, in a disconnected series of soaring leaps and tangents. Scraps of verse are blended with memories after the manner of Eliot's *Waste Land:*

> turn backward turn backward in your flight
> and make me a child again just for tonight
> good lord he's wet the bed come bring a light

The kaleidoscopic images blur and eddy in the speaker's mind and build to the memorable conclusion:

> If I could pluck
> Out of the dark that whirled
> Over the hoarse pine over the rock
> Out of the mist that furled
> Could I stretch forth like God the hand and gather
> For you my mother
> If I could pluck
> Against the dry essential of tomorrow
> To lay upon the breast that gave me suck
> Out of the dark the dark and swollen orchid of this sorrow.

These lines recapitulate the dominant imagery of the poem and rise to the intensity of the final metaphor which precisely defines the son's sense of loss.

"The Return" is almost a parable of a special kind of southern experience in the twentieth century. The narrator has fled the region of his birth, yet has felt the past sucking him down like quicksand. He is hard put to define the ambivalence of his attitude toward the South. In part, his is the plight of the deracinated intellectual; in part, the plight of the man attempting to come to terms with his personal past.

Warren's continuing concern with the theme of the past in the present gives special significance to his poem "History." His use of a flexible but firmly controlled rhyme scheme and of jagged, broken rhythms gives the poem a taut, sinewy power. At nightfall the narrator, an invader of a foreign land, stands at the head of a pass in a mountain defile looking down upon a verdant and fertile plain. On the verge of triumph, he recalls the advance through a bleak and barren wasteland. The army was confused and exhausted, but morale remained high. The intensity of the struggle, the concentration on the "prophesied" goal had given life meaning and direction. Now, poised at the moment of victory, the narrator pauses to speculate on his place in history and on the sons who will come after him:

> Our sons shall cultivate
> Peculiar crimes,
> Having not love, nor hate
> Nor memory.
> Though some,
> Of all most weary,
> Most defective of desire,
> Shall grope toward time's cold womb;
> In dim pools peer
> To see, of some grandsire,
> The long and toothéd jawbone greening there.

The dilemma described is that of a generation of men paralyzed by their spiritual vacuity. For their ancestors, time offered an opportunity for action. For themselves, time is

> the aimless bitch . . .
> Forever quartering the ground in which
> The blank and fanged
> Rough certainty lies hid.

The invader, ruminating on the search for meaning which will occupy his progeny, suddenly asks himself what is the motive of his own quest:

> We seek what end?
> The slow dynastic ease,
> Travail's cease?
> Not pleasure, sure:
> Alloy of fact?
> The act
> Alone is pure.

Submerged in the life of action, he finds the act self-justifying and self-fulfilling.

The diction and imagery of "History" carry overtones of the Israelites girding themselves to conquer the Promised Land, but the poem is distinctly contemporary in mood. The Israelite descending into the Promised Land is an allegory of the modern condition and a commentary on the American Dream. The emigrant to the New World, redeemed in action, has been replaced by the alienated modern who ransacks the past for direction and is baffled by the multiplicity of its meanings.

Closely related to "History" in their contemporaneity are two poems, companion pieces, published by Warren in the *Southern Review* (July 1935) and included in *Thirty-Six Poems*. Both mirror the unrest of the Depression years and both are grimly prophetic. The first of these, "Ransom," points to the perilous uncertainty of the times: "What wars and lecheries and the old zeal / Yet unfulfilled, unrarefied, unlaced." The poem goes on to state a problem: "Our courage needs, perhaps, new definition"; the second poem, "Letter from a Coward to a Hero," offers one solution.

The "letter" opens with a fragmented account of the hero's day, a trivial mixture of blemished triumphs and minor disappointments that make up even the days of heroes. The writer catalogues the events and adds simply: "I think you deserved better; / Therefore I am writing you this letter." The self-confessed coward muses on the childhood he shared with the hero, scraps of memory which "are hard to reconstruct," probing for the sources of the hero's strength. The writer is aware that the time is out of joint and that he is inadequate to its demands:

> Guns blaze in autumn and
> The quail falls and
> Empires collide with a bang
> That shakes the pictures where they hang
> And democracy shows signs of dry rot . . .
> But a good hunter holds the point
> And is not gun-shy;
> But I
> Am gun-shy.

The attitude of the coward toward the hero is touched with ambiguity. Though kingdoms totter and the skies fall, the hero, like the obedient hunting dog, holds the point. The comparison is calculated to flatter only the most complacent of heroes. Such courage is a virtue, but not an unalloyed one; for it is an unthinking courage, rather like a conditioned reflex.

The writer, moreover, is troubled by thoughts of the future. He hears "Drums beating for / The big war." He asks nervously, "Does the airman scream in the flaming trajectory?" He knows that the future will call for men of heroic mold, but he is concerned about the hero's qualifications. The writer continues with a stanza that defines more exactly his attitude toward his hero:

> You have been strong in love and hate.
> Disaster owns less speed than you have got,
> But he will cut across the back lot
> To lurk and lie in wait.
> Admired of children, gathered for their games,
> Disaster, like the dandelion, blooms,
> And the delicate film is fanned
> To seed the shaven lawn.

The relationship delineated is infinitely more subtle than the polarized terms *coward* and *hero* suggest. The hero, the speaker tells us, is swift and, in the race with Disaster, possesses superior speed but inferior cunning. Disaster is wily and may outwit even the strongest of heroes. Disaster's seeds are sown as casually and abundantly as those of wild flowers and may take root in the most carefully cultivated places. Like a child playing with matches, the hero plays with Disaster, oblivious to the possible consequences of his actions. The writer of the letter frankly admires the hero's courage, but his admiration is tempered by the quality of that courage. It is too innocent, too abstract. Thus, in "Letter From a Coward to a Hero" we have the first extended poetic statement of a compelling theme which Warren first explored in his biography of John Brown: the man untroubled by self-knowledge who brings disaster by his single-minded devotion to an abstract value.

A similar problem is treated in a more traditional form in one of Warren's most appealing lyrics, "The Garden," a variation on a theme by Andrew Marvell. Marvell in his great poem describes a verdant garden at the height of summer, but Warren describes a garden in early autumn when the first frost has dimmed its "summered brilliance." Now, with summer's blossoms gone, the leaves blaze with "stately flame" and the trees echo with the song of jay and cardinal. The speaker, pondering on the garden's earlier state when it was a "rank plot" of lush ripeness, imagines two lovers pausing in an arbor before they kiss, "instructed of what ripeness is." Perhaps these lovers are Adam and Eve, for as in Marvell's poem, the garden here carries suggestions of the Garden of Eden. It is an "imperial" yet natural garden ("No marbles whitely gaze among / These paths"). The sun is a "benison" and the narrator feels that "these precincts wait / In sacrament."

Marvell's garden is paradisiacal; in it man may recapture something of the innocence and spiritual wholeness he enjoyed before the Fall. Warren's garden, on the other hand, is the "ruined state" after the Fall; in it man can find not innocence but knowledge. Thus the Fall (punning on the season) is, paradoxically, a fortunate one, for from the knowledge gained of the grossness of human excess and of the power of nature for evil, man may forge a new sacramental innocence on which to be stayed. The significance for Warren of the theme of "The Garden"—that only by knowledge does man achieve his identity— may be surmised by the fact that two decades after writing the poem he restated (in a speech in 1954 at Columbia University) the theme using the same imagery: "Man can return to his lost unity, and if that return is fitful and precarious, if the foliage and flower of the innocent garden are now somewhat browned by a late season, all is the more precious for the fact, for what is now achieved has been achieved by a growth of moral awareness."

III   Eleven Poems on the Same Theme

Having explored the theme of the loss of innocence and the hope of redemption through knowledge in "The Garden," Warren turned to a more extended treatment of it in *Eleven Poems on the Same Theme*, one of "The Poet of the Month" series brought out by New Directions in 1942. This slender pamphlet is the product of a mind steeped in the tradition of English poetry. In "Bearded Oaks" Warren handles the lyric quatrain with a sensitive feeling for the traditional form yet with considerable originality of execution. The dense texture of "Love's Parable," with its staccato rhythms and faintly archaic diction, blends wit and imagination after the manner of the Metaphysicals. The dialectic of "Question and Answer" is worked out in a taut but expressive free verse. The rigorous discipline of the individual poems extends to the organization of the work as a whole. Fugal in structure, it is developed and enriched by each new variation on the central theme. *Eleven*

Poems is further integrated by recurring imagery—sun and sea, light
and dark, stone and bone—which gives an inner logic to poems widely
disparate in formal structure.

The theme of the eleven poems is stated metaphorically in the lyric
that opens the volume, "Monologue at Midnight." In it innocence is
equated with love, and knowledge with disillusion. The speaker wishes
to define himself in relation to another whom he loved and with whom
he shared "joy and innocence" and "simplicity." Their love was as
fresh as the green of the cathedral pines that sheltered it and as natural
as the progress of the seasons against which it unfolded. These memories of innocence are contaminated by the intrusion of vague overtones of guilt. Images, insubstantial and incongruous, flash into the
mind of the narrator: the lovers' shadows guiltily pursuing them, an
echo carried by the night wind, the sudden spurt of a match which
fitfully and faintly promises a moment of illumination. The narrator
can find neither substance nor definition ("And which am I and which
are you?") and concludes with a muted plea for spiritual wholeness
and integration of self: "Our mathematic yet has use / For the integers
of blessedness." His isolation and sense of loss are acute, and he is only
groping toward the formulation of the insight which Warren voices in
"Revelation" and which, in turn, becomes one of the controlling
themes of his later poetry and fiction: "In separateness only does love
learn definition."

By contrast, "Bearded Oaks," the poem that follows, describes a
moment of fulfillment, a moment poised precariously beyond the
claims of time with its inevitable involvements and contamination.
Two lovers recline in a grove of oaks. To the narrator the scene appears
submerged in water with light filtering down through layers of liquid
darkness. All motion is slowed by the denser medium, and, in this
retardation of movement, the speaker feels time itself suspended. The
lovers themselves are "twin atolls." In the depths only faint whispers
reach them of worldly processes, emphasizing the intense stillness of
the present moment and its withdrawal from time's action of "passion
and slaughter, ruth, decay. . . ." The apparent serenity of the scene
prompts the narrator to sound a positive note: "If hope is hopeless, then
fearless fear / And history is thus undone." Yet even this guarded and
tentative assertion is rendered ironic by the illusory nature of the
setting.

The submarine imagery of the scene—its suspension, as it were, in
both water and time—is evoked by the languid quality of the verse

with its heavily marked caesuras, its stately progression of sonorous open vowels, and its inversions which force a marked slowing of pace:

> The oaks, how subtle and marine,
> Bearded, and all the layered light
> Above them swims; and thus the scene,
> Recessed, awaits the positive night.
>
> So, waiting, we in the grass now lie
> Beneath the langorous tread of light:
> The grasses, kelp-like, satisfy
> The nameless motions of the air.

The elegance of "Bearded Oaks" is sustained in "Picnic Remembered" and "Love's Parable." Although structurally and metrically more formal than the other pieces in *Eleven Poems*, both lyrics extend and develop the thematic material and the imagery. In "Picnic Remembered," as in "Bearded Oaks," the lovers are suspended outside of time like "twin flies, . . . in amber tamed." The day appears "innocent" to the lovers "buoyed" like swimmers who "resign them to the flow / And pause of their unstained flood." But the sunlight which "laved" them is deceptive, for their innocence is ignorance: "we did not know / How darkness darker staired below." Similarly, in "Love's Parable" the lover rejoices in a "garden state of innocence" only to have all spoiled by the "inward sore of self."

Reading sequentially through *Eleven Poems*, it is not until we come to "Original Sin: A Short Story" that we reach an example of an idiom that Warren has made unmistakably his own. The apparent colloquial ease is achieved by piling up circumstantial details after the manner of a gifted, if rather garrulous, raconteur. The images are often macabre ("seaweed strung on the stinking stone") and the humor sardonic or cynical ("grandpa's will paid the ticket"). Abstractions ("the quantum glare of the sun") are set off against folk speech ("riding the rods"). The five-stress, iambic line is shaped and ordered by a traditional rhyme scheme, but the pattern is varied by the frequent spondees and anapests and by the use of slant rhymes.

Warren has given us a clue to the poem's intended meaning: "The story is about the personal past and the past behind the personal past, I suppose, and the problem that contemplating this past makes for us in our world of mobility and disorientation."[6] The protagonist is in flight, in part from his own past, in part from some aspect of himself connected with that past which he cannot bring himself to face. It may be, as the poem's title suggests, man's innate depravity. Restlessly searching for "a new innocence . . . to be stayed by," the protagonist cannot elude the old guilt which reappears remorselessly in a variety of guises—a nightmare, an old hound, the clock steeple in Harvard Yard. These isolated but vivid images from youth are loosed from the depths of memory and float upward into consciousness to define an apparently forgotten experience. For example:

>   . . . your grandpa, who
> Had a wen on his forehead and sat on the veranda
> To finger the precious protuberance, as was his habit to do,
> Which glinted in sun like rough garnet or the rich old brain bulging
>   through.

The speaker has more than once felt the elation of escaping from the protean and dreaded visitant; but, just at the moment his defenses are down, it reappears. At the end, the speaker becomes accommodated to a sort of self-irony. He is apparently reconciled to the now familiar experience and even finds a gloomy kind of satisfaction in the assurance that "it" will continue to haunt him.

The protagonist in "Crime," unlike the central figure in "Original Sin," has escaped the past, but insanity is the price he has had to pay for his release. The burden of guilt has become intolerable: "He cannot seem to remember . . . he is too tired to ask . . . He cannot say. . . ." The poem is an excursion into the psychology of insanity: the horrors of a diseased imagination where a tree is a "sibilant tumor," where "walls confer in the silent house," and where "eyes of pictures protrude, like a snail's, each on its prong." Yet "Crime" does not violate the thematic integrity of the volume as a whole. The killer has buried a body under the leaves, but he has forgotten the act and the victim. We are told to "envy the mad killer" because he too searches for happiness and "peace in God's eye"; his burden of guilt, unlike ours, is expiated in violence and madness. For the sane, even in an insane society, the burden remains; for "memory drips, a pipe in the cellar dark."

In "Pursuit" Warren confronts directly the issue of the disruption of the modern sensibility. He has defined the problem in the course of a discussion of the poetry of John Crowe Ransom:

The disruption of sensibility . . . has two aspects: man is a creature little lower than the angels and, at the same time, of the brute creation; again, there is a conflict between the scientific vision of quantity and that vision concerned with quality. The issue in itself is as old as man, but in the past a reconciliation has generally been possible in terms provided by a more stable way of life and a more ordered structure of ideas. The issue receives its contemporary poignancy by reason of the absence of these two things. . . . The issue is the source of Ransom's irony. The poet cannot solve his problem by an act of will, but he can attempt to work out some sort of equilibrium that may permit him, even though at odds with himself, to continue the practice of his art without violating his own honesty.[7]

Warren's own treatment of the issue in "Pursuit" is also ironic. The pursuit is more an escape into sensation and a flight from the satiety of self. The stanzas proceed by a kind of dialectic, a series of contrasts at once grotesque and romantic. The pervasive tone of illness is encountered at once in the opening reference to a hunchback who harbors his own secrets and, like a victorious general, stares silently at "you" with "imperious innocence." The "you" of the poem is in part the generalized reader, but it is also one voice of a schizoid modern self, a rather petulant and censorious superego.

The second stanza of "Pursuit" speaks in the imperative mood: "Go to the clinic. Wait in the outer room." As in the contrast of hunchback and general, the sick modern is compared to the barbarian conqueror of imperial Rome who gapes uneasily at the undaunted sacrificial fathers. But compared to the richness of the allusion, the modern man is incapable of an adequate or appropriate emotional response to his own plight and feels merely "like one who has come too late, or improperly clothed, to a party." A similar contrast develops in the third stanza. A doctor, baffled by the patient whose symptoms he cannot interpret, prescribes a trip to Florida where the frivolous search for diversion of the hypochondriac contrasts strikingly with the heroic quest of Ponce de Leon.

The modern disjunction of feeling and intellect is distilled in the conceit which opens the fifth stanza: "In Florida consider the flamingo, / Its color passion but its neck a question." And finally, as in "Original Sin," the problem revolves around the difficulty of contemplating the past: "Solution, perhaps, is public, despair personal, / But history held to your breath clouds like a mirror."

"Terror," the poem that concludes *Eleven Poems*, is quite similar to "Pursuit." Warren has given us an account of the circumstances of its composition. While spending the winter of 1939–40 in Rome on a Guggenheim grant, Warren's attention was caught by a news item in the Rome daily *Il Messaggero* announcing that United States volunteers serving in the Finnish forces then fighting Russia would not lose their citizenship. The same morning he came upon the report of the death of the chicken heart which Alexis Carrel had kept alive in his laboratory and which the sensational press had exploited in stories promising earthly immortality.

The business about the chicken heart [Warren wrote] seemed to summarize a view current in our time—that science (as popularly conceived) will solve the problem of evil by reducing it merely to a matter of "adjustment" in the physical, social, economic, and political spheres. That same day I recalled a remark made in some book by John Strachey that after science had brought "adjustment" to society it would then solve the problem of evil by bringing man a mortal immortality, by abolishing disease and death. It struck me as somewhat strange that Strachey should equate physical death and evil on a point-to-point basis, and should thereby imply that good and physical survival are identical. As for the report about the volunteers, I was struck by the thought that the same impulse which had made them go to fight Franco had made them go to fight Russia, their recent ally in Spain. That impulse officially manifested itself as a political idea, a solution for the problem of meaning in life in terms of "adjustment," but, for the purposes of the poem at least, I take a large component of that impulse to be the *passionate emptiness and tidal lust* of the modern man who, because he cannot find long-range meaning, seeks meaning in mere violence, the violence being what he wants and needs without reference ultimately to the political or other justification he may appeal to. So the two reports set us a paradox: the yearning for mere survival as meaning, and the appetite for death as meaning.[8]

The poem addresses "you," the modern man, who has been "born to no adequate definition of terror." His plight is that, blind alike to his limitations and responsibilities, he seeks restlessly to allay a gnawing, spiritual hunger. Yet nothing satisfies, neither the pleasure of the coldly passionate intellect nor the lust for physical sensation.

Since Warren was living in Rome during the composition of the poem, he was following at close quarters the efforts of Hitler and Mussolini to carve up Europe. Hence the allusions of "Terror" have a topicality not generally found in *Eleven Poems:*

> You know, by radio, how hotly the world repeats,
> When the brute crowd roars or the blunt boot-heels resound
> In the Piazza or the Wilhelmplatz. . . .

Warren has commented on the political content of the poem: "Nazism, Fascism, embody . . . the glorification of violence and death, the offer of salvation through practical success, adjustment, etc., the 'rational' state. But the boot-heels beating the stones in the Piazza or Wilhelmplatz set up echoes of the same impulses and desires across the Atlantic—all part of the same world, the same modernity."[9]

IV   Selected Poems *(1944)*

Two years after the appearance of *Eleven Poems on the Same Theme*, in the winter of 1944, Warren brought out his *Selected Poems, 1923–1943*. This collection is made up substantially of the poems which had already appeared in *Thirty-Six Poems* and in *Eleven Poems on the Same Theme*. There is, however, one important addition, "The Ballad of Billie Potts," a long and ambitious work which Warren placed first in the new edition.

For the student of Warren's work, "The Ballad of Billie Potts" is of absorbing interest, notwithstanding the fact that as a work of art it is gravely flawed. In its composition Warren set himself a problem of great difficulty—dramatizing the meaning of the past for the present. Warren's continuing efforts to solve this problem to his own satisfaction have prompted his finest work.

The subject of the ballad is drawn from the folk history of Warren's home country—a story, he tells us in the headnote, he heard as a child from an elderly relative. The facts of the tale are simple. In the early nineteenth century, Billie Potts keeps a frontier inn in the section of western Kentucky between the Tennessee and Cumberland rivers. He offers hospitality to travelers and then points them down the trail where his accomplice lies in ambush, waiting to rob and murder them. Billie Potts's son, Little Billie, sent to apprise one of his father's accomplices of the approach of an affluent traveler, attempts to kill the man himself only to be beaten to the draw and wounded. Little Billie then quarrels with his parents, journeys to the West, and after ten years returns, wealthy and complacent, to the homestead. Withholding his identity from his parents in order to "tease 'em and fun 'em," Little Billie is brutally murdered by his father who mistakes him for a rich stranger.

The narrative is related in vigorous ballad style, swiftly paced and coarsely comic. But Warren has heavily freighted this fable of the frontier with symbolism and commentary. Interspersed throughout the narrative are parenthetical sections, measured and deliberate, developing the larger implications of the story. This story is spoken by a man of the twentieth century who is watching the characters work out their destinies in frontier Kentucky and assessing the meaning of their lives for his own:

> The answer is in the back of the book but the page is gone.
> And grandma told you to tell the truth but she is dead.
> And heedless, their hairy faces fixed
> Beyond your call and question now, they move
> Under the infatuate weight of their wisdom. . . .

The effect is that of juxtaposing past and present, of generalizing the particular facts into an archetypal pattern of the discovery of guilt, the attempt at flight, and the necessity of return: "The long compulsion and the circuit hope / Back." Within the context of the American experience, the pattern is that of the westering pioneer still haunted by the tie to the heartland:

> For Time is always the new place,
> And no-place.
> For Time is always the new name and the new face,
> And no-name and no-face.
>
> For Time is motion
> For Time is innocence
> For Time is West.

There is, however, no more an escape from the past than there is an escape from the self, for the two are indivisible. Like Billie Potts, the modern man must retrace the path that he has followed, even though in seeking the source of his life he may, ironically, find death. He must understand that, in Santayana's famous phrase, the man who cannot remember the past is doomed to repeat it. Man must measure his actions and his dreams against those of all the men who have preceded him:

> And you, wanderer, back,
> For the beginning is death and the end may be life,
> For the beginning was definition and the end may be definition,
> For our innocence needs, perhaps, new definition. . . .

"A good poem," Warren has said, "is a massive, deep, and vital thing."[10] "The Ballad of Billie Potts" is such a poem, but, despite the inventiveness of its language and the sustained propulsion of its narrative, it does not come off. The mixing of manners, the folk ballad set off against the sophisticated commentary, works to the disadvantage of both by heightening the incongruity. The passages of commentary seem contrived, pretentious in their insistence on wringing profundities from what is, basically, little more than an anecdote, massive in its ironies. By contrast, the ballad seems arch and folksy.

"The Ballad of Billie Potts" does, however, point the direction toward Warren's developing interests. The opening out of the poem, the concern with narrative, suggests that Warren's gift for invention was restive under the limitations of verse and was seeking an outlet in the more ample forms of fiction. Toward the end of the 1930s he returned to the material of his first published fiction, "Prime Leaf," and, with the publication of *Night Rider* in 1939, his career as a novelist was launched.

CHAPTER 3

The Past Recaptured

ROBERT PENN WARREN'S association with the Nashville Fugitives had encouraged him to channel most of his creative energies
during the 1920s into the writing of poetry. But after his return from
Oxford in 1930, he began more and more to turn his attention to the
writing of fiction. "Prime Leaf" had opened a promising vein which
he was eager to explore further. Reminiscing about the writing of
"Prime Leaf" at Oxford, he recalled "the discovery that you could
really enjoy trying to write fiction. It was a new way of looking at
things, and my head was full of recollections of the way objects looked
in Kentucky and Tennessee. It was like going back to the age of twelve,
going fishing and all that. It was a sense of freedom and excitement."[1]

I Early Short Stories

The short stories Warren published during the 1930s are deeply
rooted in the Kentucky and Tennessee of his boyhood. As he once told
an interviewer: "It never crossed my mind when I began writing fiction that I could write about anything except life in the South. It never
crossed my mind that I knew about anything else; knew, that is, well
enough to write about. Nothing else ever nagged you enough to stir
the imagination."[2] "When the Light Gets Green," which appeared in
the *Southern Review* in 1936, is closely related in action and atmosphere to "Prime Leaf." The story concerns a small boy's recollection
of the death of his grandfather, a gallant old captain of cavalry who
had ridden with General Forrest and who had passed his declining
years reliving his campaigns with his grandson. The story poignantly
conveys the boy's awareness of the pathos of the old man's resignation
and of the puzzling emptiness of his own feelings. This youthful narrator is not unlike the shy, baffled high-school boy in "Testament of
Flood" who discovers that a classmate whom he has secretly pitied and
loved is the town harlot. Two stories that appeared in the *Virginia*

Quarterly Review during the mid-1930s also exploit southern themes and settings. "Christmas Gift" traces the growth of human understanding for a sharecropper's son by a town storekeeper and a country doctor. "Her Own People" explores the ambiguous strands of responsibility and guilt that bind a Negro maid and her white employers.[3]

These efforts at short fiction were only the by-products of a larger ambition—the writing of a novel. From 1931 until 1933 Warren was devoting such hours as he could spare from the classroom to work on *God's Own Time*, a novel dealing with life on a Kentucky farm before World War I. Eventually he became dissatisfied with it and began a second which was concerned with a small-town school, but it, too, has never been published. Then, in 1936, Warren returned to a familiar story of his youth, the uprising of tobacco farmers in Kentucky and Tennessee. To combat the tobacco trusts, the growers had formed the "Dark Tobacco District Planters' Protective Association of Kentucky and Tennessee." The first rally, in which five thousand growers took part, was called at Warren's hometown, Guthrie, Kentucky, during the autumn of 1904. When the corporations attempted to break the association by paying high prices to the farmers who did not join, the planters formed bands of "night riders" under the leadership of Dr. David A. Amoss and took the law into their own hands. The ensuing violence was climaxed by the dynamiting of company warehouses in Hopkinsville, Kentucky. Dr. Amoss was tried for the murder of a man shot from ambush during the escape, but was not convicted. Warren employed these facts as the framework of his first novel, *Night Rider*, which appeared in 1939.

II Night Rider

With his instinct for the storyteller's art, Warren begins *Night Rider* with one of the most effective means for opening a tale—a traveler on a journey. The novel's central character, Percy Munn, is wedged into the aisle of a train packed with farmers on the way to Bardsville, Kentucky, to attend a rally of an association of tobacco growers. Alone and aloof, he counters all overtures of human affection with a cold gesture of civility. The other passengers, swept to the same destination, have merged their identity into a shouting crowd which operates as a dehumanizing force, reducing them all to the mindless and all-enveloping surge of a natural catastrophe—a landslip. Percy Munn feels that his own identity is threatened by the physical presence of the crowd. He is disgusted by the "hot weight of flesh" which presses against him as the train slows for the station, and he regrets his decision to leave the seclusion of his remote tobacco farm for the spurious excitements of Bardsville. For the multitudinous human pressures of his life, he is not "braced right." Thus in the opening paragraphs of the novel, the broad outlines of Munn's character are sketched in: his indecisiveness, his sense of helplessness, and his Prufrockian revulsion from, coupled with his perverse attraction to, the coarse earthiness of life.

The plot of *Night Rider* follows with the simplicity of Greek tragedy the descending curve of Percy Munn's destruction. His life is divided between his tobacco farm, which he thinks of as "home," and his law office in Bardsville. Although only mildly interested in the formation of the Association of Growers of Dark Fired Tobacco, Munn is induced by the gruff and assertive planter Bill Christian to attend the organization meeting and then is persuaded to sit on the platform at the rally where the farmers are addressed by Senator Tolliver, a stereotyped version of the silver-tongued politician. Without warning, Munn is called out to speak. Forced to improvise, he speaks movingly of the aims of the association and is drawn to the cause by the eloquence of his own rhetoric.

These powers of persuasion make Percy Munn the natural choice to proselytize for the association among the tobacco growers, but his efforts are thwarted by small planters, rugged and stiff-necked hill folk, who doggedly refuse to sign over their crops to a board of directors. When Senator Tolliver betrays the association to the tobacco monopoly, Munn joins with Doctor MacDonald and his father-in-law, Professor Ball, in the formation of the Free Farmers' Brotherhood of Protection and Control. This euphemistic title masks a band of night riders whose tactics, reminiscent of the Ku Klux Klan, force reluctant planters into the association by destroying their crops. When even this fails, the night riders, as a last resort, blow up the warehouses of the tobacco trust.

Infected by the general moral collapse of the community, Munn is driven to murder Bunk Trevelyan, a man whose life he had once saved in court. Trevelyan had pleaded innocent to the knife murder of a neighbor whom he was known to hate and whom he had been heard to threaten. Although Trevelyan is a sullen, slovenly dirt farmer, Munn is drawn to him by his uncomplicated mind and by his readiness to act without regard to consequences. Telling himself he is motivated by an abstract desire for justice, Munn illegally searches some Negro shanties, finds a knife thought to be the murder weapon, and gains a conviction against an old Negro. Trevelyan is then induced to join the night riders, but he attempts to blackmail a member of the band by threatening to inform. Munn urges Trevelyan to flee and, when he refuses, murders him, justifying the act by reasoning that Trevelyan should have been punished for killing his neighbor.

As the night-rider movement crumbles, Doctor MacDonald is arrested on the evidence of an informer, Al Turpin, and is charged with arson and conspiracy. On the day of the trial Al Turpin is killed as he walks across the courthouse square by a shot fired by Professor Ball from Percy Munn's office window. Munn, charged with the crime, escapes to the hill farm of Willie Proudfit.

The desintegration of Munn's public life is paralleled by the collapse of his private life. His wife, May, is a bland and ineffectual woman whom Munn appears to have courted for some obscure wish to "explain himself to himself." The relationship is without either meaning or affection. The night he murders Trevelyn, Munn returns home and brutally assaults May. She leaves him, and he turns to an affair with Bill Christian's daughter, Lucille. But Lucille, too, is incapable of love and the affair ends, as did the marriage, in a loveless copulation.

Lucille Christian comes to Willie Proudfit's farm where Munn is in hiding to tell him of her father's death and to ask him to marry her. Willie learns from his bigoted and mean-spirited nephew, Sylvestus, that Lucille had come to Munn's room during the night. Rebuked by Willie, Munn leaves the farm motivated by a final expiatory act—killing Senator Tolliver, who now seems the sum of all villainy. Incapable of the deed, Munn is shot down as he flees Tolliver's house. Sylvestus had informed. Ironically, Munn is innocent of the particular acts for which he dies. Sylvestus was mistaken in believing that Munn had committed adultery with Lucille at Willie's house, yet Munn is an adulterer. Similarly, Munn is not guilty of the murder of Al Turpin for which the posse kills him, yet Munn is a murderer.

Such a summary of the plot, while it calls attention to the directness of the narrative line and the skillful handling of the irony, fails to do justice to the thematic richness of *Night Rider*. Percy Munn is the prototype of the most familiar of all Warren characters. He is a man obsessed with the need to know himself, to plumb the "darkly coiling depth within himself" (162). He longs for self-definition, for what he called the "unifying fulfillment" (208). His actions spring from his awareness that he is a divided man and from his longing for identity,

for integration of self. His life resembles the stereopticon of his childhood. Gazing through the lenses, he had seen a "rich, three-dimen-
sional little world. . . . He had felt that if he could just break through
into that little world . . . he would know the most unutterable bliss."
He cannot, however, superimpose the fragmented elements of his
nature. His life is without depth and substance, like the stereopticon
cards held in his hand, "the flat, dull, fading picture printed in dupli-
cate" (161).

The sense of alienation is heavy upon him. He seizes desperately
upon a warm human gesture, a sympathetic face in a crowd or a word
of appreciation, for he longs to understand fully another human being
and hence himself. When he hears the speech and song of men par-
taking warmly of their common humanity, he is torn between his sudden heightened awareness of human brotherhood and his sense of deprivation at being powerless to share it.

Percy Munn's numbed sensibilities are equaled by his paralysis of
the will. He longs to realize himself in action, but he is unwittingly
shaped by the stronger wills about him. Invited to join the board of
directors of the association, he instinctively blurts out "no!"—but he
joins. Asked to scrape plant beds with the night riders, he replies: "It
just isn't in me, I reckon"—but he scrapes them. When he is confronted with an account in the newspapers of events in which he was
involved, he feels "as if he were reading of something in which he had
had no part" (173). When he does act, it is action disengaged from
thought as when he impulsively punches a man who jokingly implied
that Munn had rigged a jury.

The duality of Munn's nature is dramatized in *Night Rider* by Warren's handling of the imagery of darkness and light. Night and day
reveal the two aspects of Munn's character which are ultimately irreconcilable: "He thought how the night may be, in truth, mirror to the
day, returning the reflection of a man's self to him twisted and confused and almost unrecognizable like the reflection in a flawed, pocked,
and dirty glass, or in those contorting mirrors you see in tent shows, or
in disturbed water" (177). The opening scenes of the novel are bathed
in blazing sunlight, but Percy Munn, a man "locked inside the darkness
that [is] himself," instinctively seeks out the shadows (177). He prefers
the darkened privacy of his hotel room in Bardsville, the cool gloom of
the stables, and the dim obscurity of the tobacco barns. Early in the
novel he marvels that "night changed everything, even the most accustomed landscape, your own fields. Or the face of somebody you knew

and loved" (149). He secretly studies the face of his wife in sleep, hoping to find something that will explain either her or, by reflection, himself.

Munn seems most at ease by night, for the bright blue vault of the sky stirs uneasy speculations in him. It is a vast emptiness and hollowness under which he finds no comfort or serenity. At the end of the first day of proselytizing for the association, he finds solace in the "comfort of the night and isolation" (41). As his involvement with the association increases, his mind seems like an "eye unseeing but straining forward into the dark" (46). Munn's first illegal action, the shakedown of the Negro cabins, takes place under the "uneven light of the moon," and a deepening darkness closes over the novel as it moves toward its conclusion.

The pivotal scene of *Night Rider* is the one in which Munn takes the oath of the Brotherhood for Protection and Control. To join the night riders, Munn must ride to an abandoned sawmill deep in the woods. In the "dark shadow" that envelops the mill, men stand alone, mute, suspicious, their faces only a "whitish blur." When Munn hears his name called to summon him to the mill, he is startled at the strangeness of the sound of the familiar word. He enters the "blacker, interior darkness" of the mill, gropes unseeingly down a black corridor, only to be thrust suddenly into a room brilliantly illuminated by the beam from a reflector lantern. Physically blinded by the glare, the equivalent of the moral blindness of the act he will perform, Munn takes the oath:

"Come forward," the voice said, and he walked across the intervening ten feet or so of floor toward the lantern and the voice. He passed beyond the range of the lantern's rays, was completely blind for an instant before his eyes could accustom themselves to the dark, and then saw the man standing behind the table that supported the lantern, and the other men sitting on benches and boxes beyond. (156)

Munn's decision to embark on a career of violence and lawlessness is the central and irrevocable action of his life—from this act all else follows. The significance of the action is heightened and focused by the movement from light to darkness, the dominant pattern of imagery of the novel.

As Munn's despair deepens, his actions seem to him like the "blows of a blind man who strikes out at the undefined sounds which penetrate his private darkness." His mind grazes off tangentially from the issue at hand to a "confused darkness of speculation." With the ultimate violence, the dynamiting of the company warehouses, Munn believes "it will all be different. It will all be clear as day." But this too fails, and eventually he becomes a creature of the night, cowering like an animal in his cave, afraid to venture into the light. The final scene of the novel, the final sentence, reinforces and resolves this night symbolism. Stumbling with plunging strides, Munn runs for the "woods, the absorbing darkness." Shot down, he hears, "so empty in the darkness," the shouts of his pursuers, "like the voices of boys at a game in the dark."

Warren's development of the two women in Percy Munn's life, his wife, May, and his mistress, Lucille Christian, further emphasizes both the symbolic pattern of darkness and light and the deep-seated division of self. Whereas he sees May generally in brilliant sunshine in her garden or in a meadow, he knows Lucille only in the dark. When she comes to him for the last time, Lucille recalls the fact to him: "You know, we've never talked, not really talked, you and me, in the light" (435). Munn first sees Lucille standing "in complete stillness, in absorbed repose," and he, mistaking the appearance for the reality, hopes to find in her the serenity of spirit for which he longs. She stimulates his "appetite for definition, for certainty" (251). Yet Lucille has sought the same thing in Percy Munn, for she too has a divided nature:

> She was, it seemed to him, two persons. There was the person who came to his room, and stood with one finger to her lips while she gently pushed the shadowy white door shut behind her; and there was the person whom he saw moving about the house in the daytime, talking casually and easily to him or her father. . . . The two persons seemed quite distinct to him. (240–41)

Lucille also longs for the unifying fulfillment. She tells Munn, echoing his own words earlier in the novel, "If everything, everything you were and wanted and owed to people—everything—matched up just once, even for just a minute so you were really one person, completely, then you would be almost too happy to live" (241).

Among the characters in *Night Rider*, only the enigmatic Captain Todd seems to possess the "inner certainty of self" (43) for which Percy Munn and Lucille Christian hunger. Captain Todd has about him the air of conviction and confidence which Munn attributes to his life of action. Todd had heroically fought the Yankees during the Civil War, and after Appomattox he had captured and summarily hanged the bushwhackers and guerrillas who preyed on a defeated and demoralized South. But whatever the source of the captain's "ripe, secret security," it remains hidden behind a mask of amiable gravity.

The possibility of fulfillment in action which Munn finds so compelling in the life of Captain Todd also attracts him to Willie Proudfit, the farmer at whose home he hides after his escape from Bardsville. In the closing pages of the novel, Willie tells his story, a tour de force of dialect narrative at which Warren excels. Proudfit had traveled West, alone, killing buffalo and fighting Indians. He had wrested from the wilderness a confidence in himself which he cannot articulate but which he manifests in the actions of his life. Like Captain Todd, Proudfit has won from the past a meaning, and he recounts his life with modesty but with a consciousness of its significance.

The contrast with Percy Munn's life is extreme. Munn had traveled East to study law and to spend his afternoons reading fragmentary and irrelevant items from the newspapers to an elderly and eccentric cousin, Miss Ianthe Sprague. She has no recollection of the past nor any desire to remember it, "for out of memory rises the notion of a positive and purposive future, the revision of the past" (212). Integration of self is dependent on a sense of continuity with the past and faith in the future. But Munn, like Miss Sprague, must "protect himself by denying memory, as it were, from the contact of the self he had been. And his mind closed like a valve against all thoughts of the future" (219). The lesson Willie Proudfit learned from the past, salvation through righteousness, makes no impression on Munn. Quite the contrary, he leaves the farm for a final act of vengeance, the murder of Senator Tolliver.

Related to Munn's failure to grasp the meaning of the past for the present is his besetting sin of abstraction. For Munn the association becomes the idea incarnate, a means to salvation beyond the flux of history. His first speech to the farmers dramatizes the force of the idea: "There is nothing here but an idea" (26). And later, "The Association, that was what he was now, if he was anything." He feels at last that his allegiance to the idea and his thirst for action will be realized in a single moment of truth, the dynamiting of the company warehouses— "that reeling moment of certainty and fulfillment." But even the immaculate idea is at the mercy of human inadequacy. At the trial of Doctor MacDonald the act of violence is analyzed and dissected, and the Truth becomes not a thing indivisible, but the multiple truths of the many fallible human beings who are involved: "The truths of those people were not the truth that had been his that night; but truth was his no longer. The truth: it devoured and blotted out each particular truth, each individual man's truth, it crushed truths as under a blundering tread, it was blind" (365).

Night Rider is a remarkably mature first novel. In it Warren has created a complete fictional world, a world of substance and texture which is coherent and self-contained. His delight in action and suspense and his variety of characterization are already clearly apparent, but in the Warren canon the novel now appears rigidly formalistic, schematic in structure, and restrained in style. Warren did take a calculated risk in choosing Percy Munn for his center of consciousness. In telling the story from the point of view of a befuddled and divided character, he might have blurred his effects and left the meaning of his work ultimately obscure. In 1935 in an essay on Thomas Wolfe, Warren complained that *Of Time and the River* had no organizing principle, no clearly delineated character at the center of the novel to give the raw materials of Wolfe's personal experience design and direction:

> It may be objected that other works of literary art, and very great ones at that, have heroes who defy definition and who are merely centers of "fury." For instance, there is Hamlet or Lear. But a difference may be observed. Those characters may defy the attempt at central definition, but the play hangs together in each case as a structure without such definition; that is, there has been no confusion between the sensibility that produced the play as an object of art, and the sensibility of a hero in a play.[4]

No such confusion is evident in *Night Rider*. In fact, Warren's detachment from his hero is clear, notably in his habit of referring to him throughout the novel as *Mr*. Munn. Because Munn does defy central definition, his remoteness from the reader is the significant thing about him. He is equally remote from himself and from his world— he is one of the hollow men. But since we see the story from his point of view, we must infer this hollowness from the complex of situations and relationships which constitutes the structure of the novel. The effect is difficult to achieve, and Warren may have felt that he was only partially successful; for in his second novel, *At Heaven's Gate*, he experimented with a more varied handling of the angle of vision than that employed in *Night Rider*.

After *Night Rider* appeared, Warren was surprised at the persistence of the impression that he was writing "historical fiction." Eighteen years after its publication, in 1957, he told Ralph Ellison:

I remember the troops coming in when martial law was declared in that part of Kentucky. When I wrote *Night Rider* I wasn't thinking of it as history. For one thing, the world it treated still, in a way, survived. You could still talk to the old men who had been involved. In the 1930's I remember going to see a judge down in Kentucky—he was an elderly man then, a man of the highest integrity and reputation—who had lived through that period and who by common repute had been mixed up in it—his father had been a tobacco grower. He got to talking about that period in Kentucky. He said, "Well, I won't say who was and wasn't mixed up in some of those things, but I will make one observation: I have noticed that the sons of those who were opposed to getting a fair price for tobacco ended up as either bootleggers or brokers." But he was an old-fashioned kind of guy, for whom bootlegging and brokerage looked very much alike. Such a man didn't look "historical" thirty years ago. Now he looks like the thigh bone of a mastodon.[5]

Twenty years later, in 1977, Warren was still trying to correct the record. "I'm sometimes said to be an historical novelist," he told an interviewer. "The first one was *Night Rider*, about the tobacco wars when I was a child, and I saw it, so I guess that's not history. . . . And also the novel about Nashville in the thirties, *At Heaven's Gate*—it wasn't history then. I was living there when I was twenty-five years old, and I was seeing those same things happen. . . . They were coming out of the world I lived in, but not an historical one."[6]

III   At Heaven's Gate

Upon its publication in 1943 *At Heaven's Gate* prompted a certain amount of speculation concerning its sources in Warren's experience. Malcolm Cowley professed to see in the city which is the locus of the novel a thinly disguised Nashville, Tennessee, "with a few traits borrowed from Memphis." The university, he thought, might be Vanderbilt and the group of intellectuals the Fugitives. As for the finance capitalist at the center of the novel, Bogan Murdock, Cowley found him reminiscent of Colonel Luke Lee, a former United States Senator and securities manipulator who went to jail for his part in the collapse of a Nashville bank.[7]

But to label *At Heaven's Gate* a *roman à clef* would be to undervalue a powerful and intricately wrought work of art, forceful in style and filled with scenes freshly observed and vividly rendered. Warren has given us a clue to the importance he attributes to his conception. It was Dante's Seventh Circle, he tells us, "that provided, with some liberties of interpretation and extension, the basic scheme and meta-

phor for the whole novel. All of the main characters are violators of
nature." The businessman hero, Bogan Murdock, "was supposed to
embody, in one of his dimensions, the desiccating abstraction of power,
to be a violator of nature, a usurer of Dante's Seventh Circle, and to
try to fulfill vicariously his natural emptiness by exercising power over
those around him."[8] The novel is unique among Warren's novels in
that it was written from an elaborate outline. "I had about an eighty-
page synopsis—almost paragraph by paragraph—of what I wanted to
get accomplished in that novel. . . . I spent a year or two in the plan-
ning. . . . I had a bitter time trying to feel fresh on the things that I had
already planned out so carefully, that looked so beautiful in the plan."[9]

The house of Murdock is, like Faulkner's Sartoris clan, a family in
decline. Bogan Murdock can trace his ancestry to Andrew Jackson, and
a portrait of the Old Hero hangs on the wall in the Murdock library.
Bogan's father, Major Lemuel Murdock, "fought four bitter years for
the defense and honor of his native state" (133). Then, in defense of
his own "honor," he murdered his opponent in a gubernatorial election
for charging, accurately, that Murdock had worked hand in glove with
carpetbaggers. Bogan himself has risen to wealth and influence through
the manipulation of securities, which, he admits in a moment of crisis,
is "decidedly illegal" (344). Bogan's wife, Dorothy, boasts a great-
great-grandfather who was a general in the American Revolution and
a grandfather who was a senator in the Confederate Congress. Her
father, however, died a failure; and Dorothy is, as her husband sums
her up, a "drunken, sodden, self-abusing, middle-aged bitch" (347).

Bogan Murdock has created a world by the sheer force of superior
personality, a "special type of subtle pressure" (249). He uses politeness
as other men use force; as his daughter, Sue, says, "It's just a way of
making people do things" (6). Murdock's gift is a cold detachment
from and an understanding of the ways of men. He analyzes college
football with the same passionless objectivity he employs in his business
deals, and his justification of professionalism in collegiate athletics is
the same as his rationale for the juggling of stocks and bonds: " . . .
since we do not enjoy the satisfaction of virtue, we might at least enjoy
the satisfaction of efficiency" (20). He can discover no irony in justifying his own conduct by quoting the Emperor Tiberius. The reader
never enters the consciousness of Bogan Murdock. He is seen from several discrete points of view, but chiefly through the eyes of two people
who fall fatally under his spell: Jerry Calhoun, who willingly and grate-
fully comes under his influence and is destroyed by it, and Murdock's
daughter, Sue, who is destroyed by her efforts to rebel from it.

When he first enters the world of Bogan Murdock, Jerry Calhoun
appears to be a "kindly, humble monster." Sue Murdock, coming upon
him in her father's living room, wonders "where in the world he had
come from" (40). The world out of which Jerry came is certainly the
opposite of Sue Murdock's world. His mother died at his birth, and his
father is a clumsy, inept dirt farmer whom his son considers a failure.
His Uncle Lew, a waspish and clubfooted misanthrope, seems to Jerry
like the images the old man carves from peach stones, "not animal and
not quite human" (45). His great-aunt Ursula sits blind and dirty in a
corner rocker, waited on by an aged and incompetent Negro house-
keeper. Jerry's youth seems to him, in retrospect, "ugly, monotonous,
fumbling, and dirty" (52).

Jerry's prowess as an All-American at the university calls him to the
attention of Bogan Murdock, whose world represents to Jerry an escape
from the ugliness and poverty of his youth. Murdock's corruption of
Jerry is subtly conceived. He joins a fraternity, allowing an "anonymous alumnus" to pay his initiation fee. Offered a job selling bonds in
Murdock's firm, Jerry instantly rejects a graduate fellowship at the
university. Murdock himself adds the finishing touches: trips to New
York to rub off the provincial edges, invitations to ride to hounds, the
address of the right tailor, election to the right clubs.

At Murdock's suggestion, Jerry submits himself to the tutorials of an
eccentric economist, Duckfoot Blake. Blake's advice on the methods of
selling bonds, given ironically, is accepted humorlessly by Jerry as gospel. Blake's house where they frequently work is sufficiently reminiscent of Jerry's own house to fill him with "discomfort and revulsion"
(79). Yet there is a part of him which clings nostalgically to the memories of his earlier life which, in comparison with his present sophisti-
cation, seems uncomplicated and uncluttered.

Jerry's divided attitude toward Blake's house and his own is but the
symptom of a deeper division within himself. "It was," he thinks, "like
there were two Jerry Calhouns, the Jerry Calhoun to whom it had happened and the Jerry Calhoun to whom nothing had happened" (232).
He finds himself baffled and lost in the "vast conspiracy" of the world
(31). He achieves the goal which all of "Murdock's boys" long for,
engagement to the "Infanta," Sue Murdock, but is later rejected by her
as an inferior version, if not an agent, of her father. At such moments
of crisis, he can only repeat his name like some talismanic device which
may evoke the reality which is himself: "Jerry Calhoun, who was Jerry
Calhoun, who was Jerry—" (34).

Sue Murdock dismisses Jerry because she understands his weakness but not her own. "Oh, you'll die rich," she tells him, but "you're an emotional cripple" (99). Sue, too, is emotionally crippled, for she has little knowledge of what she is or of what she wants. A beautiful, spoiled woman, she offers no defense for her conduct beyond an insistence on her immediate desires. When her brother inquires why she jilted Jerry, she answers, "Because I wanted to" (209). When Slim Sarrett, a student at the university, suggests she become a writer, she replies, "I don't want to be." When Sarrett attempts to analyze the "special complex of forces represented by the word *want*," Sue is not interested (147). For her "it's a damned good reason" (209). She acts, Jerry observes, "like the minute was all there was, like there wasn't any tomorrow, or like what yesterday was or tomorrow would be didn't have any connection" (117). Fitfully interested in the theater, Sue feels most alive when impersonating another. After leaving Jerry, she feels like an actress rehearsing a part, "beautiful and empty like a dream" (152). "Oh, what am I?" she asks, and her cry is echoed by her mother's "I don't know what I am" (185).

Sue's life is a cycle of things desperately desired and, once obtained, just as desperately despised: a Northern finishing school, her debut, Jerry Calhoun, escape from her father. It is this last which drives her to impetuous and spectacular extremes of conduct. Unlike Jerry Calhoun, who only spasmodically and dimly grasps the fact that he hates his father because he wishes to be free of the past which the older man represents, Sue quite frankly despises her father and violently rejects him. Of her father she says: "Because he made me he thinks he owns me." Her cry epitomizes the plight of all who populate Bogan Murdock's world, for he did make them what they are and he exacts an unswerving allegiance.

Both Jerry and Sue come to grief in their efforts to cope with the world of Bogan Murdock. Jerry ends in jail as the scapegoat in the collapse of Murdock's financial empire. Sue drifts restlessly from man to man, finding in each some haunting resemblance to her hated father. After breaking her engagement to Jerry, she becomes the mistress of Slim Sarrett, a graduate student, boxer, and poet. She leaves him and enters into a sordid liaison with Jason Sweetwater, a union official dedicated to breaking the power of Bogan Murdock. Pregnant with Sweetwater's child, Sue undergoes an abortion; and, while recovering in her apartment, she is strangled by the crazed Sarrett.

Earlier in the novel Sarrett, in the presence of Sue, had exposed Murdock's fundamental flaw: "You . . . represent to me the special disease of our time, the abstract passion for power, a vanity springing from an awareness of the emptiness and unreality of the self which can only attempt to become real and human by the oppression of people who manage to retain some shreds of reality and humanity" (250). Slim Sarrett understands the motives of Bogan Murdock for he shares them—his passion for power is equally insatiable. In the dialogue between Slim and Sue which opens the novel, Slim can see no reason for riding a horse. It is too easy to master a brute beast; "the true contest should be to set oneself against another human being" (4).

Like Bogan Murdock, Slim has created a world by the magnetism of his own personality, a world which is centered in his studio-apartment. He prepares the introduction of each new person "as scrupulously and as cunningly as a dramatist prepares the entrance of a hero" (204). For Slim art, not finance, is the central reality. He speaks grandly of his role, for he is pretentiously, self-consciously the *artist:* "An artist, a poet, never feels the need to 'make-up' anything. . . . He finds in facts ample occupation, and he can afford to face them. . . . The artist is the enemy of blur" (150). Yet his art is as desiccated, abstract, and sterile in its own way as Murdock's finance. To men like Duckfoot Blake, it is a "conspiracy among introverts . . . and intellectual tat-and-crochet boys" (203). And despite Slim's insistence that the artist does not need to "make up" anything, his own life is an enormous lie. His world collapses when, at the height of a party at his studio, Billie Constantidopeles, an old friend, appears unexpectedly to reveal that Slim's father was not a riverboat captain blown up under picturesque circumstances but a vacuum-cleaner salesman from Georgia and that Slim is a homosexual.

Slim's sickness, like Jerry Calhoun's, is a disruption of sensibility. But unlike Jerry, Slim cultivates and savors the duality of his nature. He boasts of leading a "double life which every artist is forced by his nature to lead" (165). Vain of his reputation as both college boxer and poet, he makes no effort to integrate his several roles: "I happen to prefer to keep my special physical discipline disjunct from my esthetic discipline—from my poetry" (102). This inner division is further emphasized by Slim's sexual ambivalence.

Slim has a compulsive, voyeuristic obsession to analyze other people, for he knows that they talk about themselves out of a desire to define themselves. His own poetry is such a dialogue. It is Slim who, in a seminar paper, articulates the quest of all the major characters of the novel—each is groping toward some kind of self-knowledge:

"The tragic flaw in the Shakesperean hero is a defect in self-knowledge. . . .
Bacon wrote: Knowledge is power. Bacon was thinking of knowledge of the
mechanisms of the external world. Shakespeare wrote: Self-knowledge is
power. Shakespeare was thinking of the mechanisms of the spirit, to which
the mechanisms of the external world, including other persons, are instru-
ments. In other words, Shakespeare was interested in success. By success, he
meant: Self-fulfillment. But his tragedy is concerned with failure. Naturally.
The successful man . . . offers only the smooth surface, like an egg. In so far
as he is truly successful, he has no story. He is pure. But poetry is concerned
only with failure, distortion, imbalance—with impurity. And poetry itself is
impurity. The pure cry of pain is not poetry. The pure gasp and sigh of love
is not poetry. Poetry is the impurity which an active being secretes to become
pure. It is the glitter of pus, richer than Ind, the monument in dung, the
oyster's pearl." (196)

The worlds of Bogan Murdock and Slim Sarrett constitute the two
worlds of the novel. Characters who are at home in one world are ill
at ease in the other. Slim and Rosemary, a crippled student at the university whom Sue has befriended, are hopelessly out of place when
invited to the Murdock estate. Similarly, Jerry and Bogan's son, Ham-
mond, are equally misplaced in Slim's bohemian studio. In a symbolic
scene, Bogan Murdock and Slim Sarrett confront one another in Sue's
apartment. Forced to choose between them, Sue exchanges one world
for another but cannot survive the change. She is outraged by her
father's world; she is murdered by Sarrett when she rejects his world.

Two characters in *At Heaven's Gate* move easily between these two
worlds and link them together. Both are men whose self-knowledge
makes them at home in any world. Jason Sweetwater has made his
work his life: "A man could not believe in himself unless he believed
in something else"—such is the sum of his wisdom. And Sweetwater
understands Slim Sarrett: "He is a liar just like a channel catfish ain't
a canary. He swims in a lie, and he is in the lie and the lie is in him. . . .
He lives in a dream world" (303–304). And there is Duckfoot Blake,
who in his breezy cynicism and wisecracking speech looks forward to
Jack Burden in *All the King's Men*. Duckfoot finds the same unreality
principle in Bogan Murdock that Sweetwater finds in Slim Sarrett:
"Bogan Murdock is just a dream Bogan Murdock had, a great big won-
derful dream" (373). Duckfoot, like Sweetwater, has won from adversity a measure of affirmation, the knowledge that "everything he had
ever done or said or thought mattered" (372).

Set off against the worlds of Murdock and Sarrett is yet another world of the novel, that of Ashby Wyndham. In intercalary chapters throughout *At Heaven's Gate*, Warren has introduced the "Statement of Ashby Wyndham," a narrative cast in the form of a condemned man's confession. The story, at first apparently unrelated to the main narrative, converges on it slowly but inevitably like the superimposed images of a rangefinder, giving depth and dimension to the themes of the novel. Ashby Porsum Wyndham is a headstrong, semiliterate backwoods farmer. Having sinned against his brother, he undergoes a spiritual conversion when he has a vision of his dead infant son. He starts down the river on a houseboat, stopping at towns to preach the gospel to all who will listen. He and his disciples arrive eventually at the city which is the setting of the novel. Ashby's spiritual pride leads him to destroy, one by one, the lives of those around him. His flaw is a defect in self-knowledge, and his plight is genuinely tragic. He, too, builds a world by the eloquence of his tongue and the force of his will, only to see it collapse as a result of his overweening drive for power over others. His story cuts across the main line of the narrative at a point where his cousin, Private Porsum, a hero of World War I and a Murdock puppet, finds himself fatally compromised by his involvement in Murdock's financial schemes. Reading Ashby's confession, Porsum repents and breaks with Murdock, the act that brings Murdock's empire crashing down.

Like Willie Proudfit of *Night Rider*, Ashby Wyndham has confronted his past and has come to terms with it. In so doing, he stands in marked contrast to most of the other characters of the novel, who, like Percy Munn, deny the past or fail to grasp its meaning. Sue Murdock will not admit the past's claim upon her. Jerry Calhoun has "shut his mind resolutely to any thought of the past" (22), and in a final moment of illumination he must face the fact that he wanted the people who shared that past—Aunt Ursula, Uncle Lew, even his father—dead. Bogan Murdock and Slim Sarrett repudiate the past by rejecting their real fathers and creating imaginary fathers that satisfy their image of themselves. Jason Sweetwater and Duckfoot Blake stand apart from these characters in their acceptance of the past, symbolized by their acceptance of their fathers.

The evangelical Christianity of Ashby Wyndham and the rather bleak affirmations of Sweetwater and Blake are the only positive notes of a novel in which the pervasive tone is nihilistic. The act of love is either blindly compulsive or coldly analytic. "I don't love anybody," Sue cries, and her words are echoed by her mother's "I don't love anything." Images of decay and disease, reminiscent of Warren's use of motifs from *The Waste Land* in his early poetry, dominate the novel. There is the unremitting commentary of Uncle Lew, who speaks of Lemuel Murdock as a "murdering blackguard swole with pride pus." Jason Sweetwater observes that a man has got "to boil the pus out." Slim Sarrett is concerned with the "dung and offal" which fertilize his art.

Warren's use of Eliotic imagery calls attention to the various literary influences to which he was responding and which are reflected in *At Heaven's Gate*. In speaking of his first two novels, Warren has said that "there was a good deal of the shadow not only of the events of that period but of the fiction of that period."[10] But influence hunting, always dangerous, is especially perilous in the case of Warren. Few writers of our time have been more sensitive to the shaping power of the literary tradition and perhaps none has read more widely and deeply.

At Heaven's Gate, set as it is in the 1920s, inevitably invites comparison with the novels which have shaped our picture of that decade. Warren has said that the young people about whom F. Scott Fitzgerald wrote "were groping to find some satisfaction in a world from which the old values had been withdrawn."[11] The same could be said of the young people of *At Heaven's Gate*, the beautiful and damned. The tone of postwar disenchantment that pervades Fitzgerald's fiction, the pathos of mangled and dislocated lives, Warren also found in his reading of Ernest Hemingway. Warren learned from Hemingway how to express compassion without stating it baldly. And occasionally the staccato, understated Hemingway manner insinuates itself into the dialogue of *At Heaven's Gate*.

It is, however, Warren's fellow southerner William Faulkner whom he most closely resembles in both manner and matter. Warren, we know, followed Faulkner's career closely and admiringly—his essay in appreciation is an incisive critique of Faulkner's work.[12] Their fiction has much in common: the lush rhetoric, the brooding meditations on the past, the exploitation of the traditional order for its symbolic value in the present. In philosophical weight and tragic intensity Faulkner goes beyond Warren, just as he goes beyond all other American writers of this century. But Warren's knowledge of the variety of contemporary life, particularly his knowledge of regions outside the South, has given his work a broader scope than Faulkner allowed himself.

IV   *Naturalism and Symbolism in Warren's Novels*

More profitable than searching for point-by-point influences in Warren's fiction is seeing his work against the two dominant literary tendencies of the time—Naturalism and Symbolism. For a definition of
Naturalism we can turn to Warren himself, who defined it in the
course of a discussion of T. S. Stribling: "The naturalist novelist took
science as the source of his method and his philosophy. His method
was, professedly, objective and transcriptive; he was concerned with
fact, not value. Motivation of human conduct was to be understood in
terms of biology, biochemistry and such."[13]

It would do violence to Warren's fiction to try to force it into such
a straitjacket as this, but both *Night Rider* and *At Heaven's Gate*
exhibit much of Naturalistic theory and method. Both are big books
filled with panoramic scenes. In *Night Rider* Warren utilizes the characteristic milieu of the Naturalistic novel in which man becomes a
hunted and tortured animal. In *At Heaven's Gate* atavistic impulses
lurk just below the thin veneer of civilized behavior. The attention to
social class, ranging in *At Heaven's Gate* from financier to dirt farmer,
suggests the slice-of-life so admired by the early Naturalists. An amply
documented picture of society is occasionally described in a scientific
terminology drawn particularly from chemistry and physiology. In
both novels the central characters find themselves in the familiar Naturalistic predicament: the individual submerged by social forces which
he only dimly understands and which he is powerless to control. These
Naturalistic elements in Warren's first two novels link them to a distinguished American tradition which includes the work of Frank Norris,
Theodore Dreiser, and Sherwood Anderson.

With certain tendencies of the Naturalists, however, Warren is
clearly out of sympathy, notably with their notorious hostility to literary form—a resistance stemming from their belief that, since life is
patternless, a plot must be a violation of truth. Warren's characters are
molded by their pasts, but he never succumbs to a simplistic reliance
on heredity and environment to explain human conduct. Certainly the
materialism of the Naturalists, what Warren has called the "vision of
the God-abandoned and sanction-stripped world of natural process,"[14]
had little imaginative appeal for him.

Developing parallel to Naturalism was Symbolism, a tradition
widely at variance with Naturalism in its aims and methods. Opposed

to the Naturalist's tendency to adopt a mechanistic view of nature and a social conception of man is the Symbolist's tendency to stress an organic view of nature and the individuality of man. The Naturalist turns outward to the external world to observe life with objectivity and to record it in the impersonal language of science. The Symbolist turns inward on his own ego to savor what in his nature is idiosyncratic. He consequently finds himself troubled with a problem of communication. Since his feelings and emotions are unique, he must invent a new language to convey his uniqueness. Although such a language will necessarily be private and difficult, working more by suggestion and intimation than by direct expression, this very imprecision may be a source of strength. The Symbolic novel has an aura of uncertainty which, paradoxically, may charge the work with a vibrant sense of reality. It has an extra dimension, an imaginative margin of ambiguity which adds emotional resonance and artistic power. Warren seems to have had some such idea in mind when he spoke of "that feeling of a mysterious depth which is one of the chief beauties of the art" of fiction.[15] His use of the richly suggestive symbolism of light and dark in *Night Rider* and of disease and decay in *At Heaven's Gate* gives these works a heightened meaning that is unavailable to the doctrinaire naturalist.

Edmund Wilson has said that "the literary history of our time is to a great extent that of the development of Symbolism and of its fusion or conflict with Naturalism."[16] In *Night Rider* and *At Heaven's Gate* Warren demonstrates how both of these traditions might be exploited. In his third novel, *All the King's Men,* he fuses them powerfully and imaginatively, the one reinforcing the other. The result is one of the great novels of twentieth-century American literature.

CHAPTER 4

The Past and Its Burden

THE idea for the work which eventually developed into *All the King's Men* came to Robert Penn Warren during the winter of 1937–38 while he was teaching at Louisiana State University. As his starkly prophetic poems of that period reveal, Warren was meditating on the principles of decency and democracy and their capacity to survive in the face of deepening economic crisis at home and rampant nationalism abroad. The time seemed to him, as he said later, "a period of unmasking of blank power."[1] His conception for the projected work centered on a dictatorial Southern politician whose motives, though prompted by idealism, are corrupted by the abuse of power. Warren was drawn to the paradox of the politician whose wellspring of power is his ability to satisfy vicariously the needs of the people he governs but whose exercise of that power leads him to the discovery of his moral hollowness. Senator Tolliver of *Night Rider,* sucking vitality from the anonymous crowds he addresses, is a preliminary sketch for such a figure.

Warren first planned a verse play, and the original version entitled *Proud Flesh* was written chiefly in Rome in 1939.[2] But he was dissatisfied with the work in dramatic form and abandoned it as he became increasingly absorbed in *At Heaven's Gate.* The two works are, however, related thematically. In a preface to *All the King's Men* written in 1953, Warren said that the novel was "a continuation of the experience of writing *At Heaven's Gate,* just as that novel had been, in a way, a continuation of *Proud Flesh.*"[3] This thematic continuity is in part owing to Warren's habit of keeping several works in progress simultaneously. "I generally carry several novels around in me," he told Harvey Breit. "I have to carry things around for so long that they're all overlapping."[4]

I   All the King's Men *and Huey Long*

When *All the King's Men* appeared in 1946, the reviewers seized immediately upon its resemblance to Huey P. Long and his political regime in Louisiana. Long was the dominant figure in southern politics while Warren was teaching at Memphis and Nashville during the early 1930s, and after moving to Louisiana State University in 1934, he had the opportunity to observe the results of Longism at first hand. But just as the intervening years have made the novel's debt to the Long legend seem the least important thing about it, so the importance of Long himself has dwindled in the perspective of history. The shenanigans of the Louisiana Kingfish seem less ominous than they once did. It is difficult now to recreate the mood of Depression-era Louisiana when young and desperate men lay by the roadside armed with shotguns waiting to open fire on Huey Long's state troopers, a personal army known as "Huey's Cossacks."[5] The southern dictator who travestied democratic processes has been metamorphosed into a folk figure, part comic bumpkin and part homespun philosopher after the manner of a southern Will Rogers.

The biblical allusions in Huey Long's speeches not only gave an evangelical quality to his drive for power but also testified to his devout training in a Baptist home in the piny woods region of north-central Louisiana. Long married at nineteen, worked as a traveling salesman to support himself and his wife, and, incredibly, completed a three-year course at Tulane Law School in eight months. By turns cunning and candid, belligerent and vindictive, he systematically and skillfully built a monolithic political machine which placed him in the Louisiana governor's chair by the time he was thirty-five. With a growing squad of bodyguards hovering in the background, he survived physical assaults, political attacks, and impeachment proceedings until, when the voters sent him to the United States Senate in 1932, he was the undisputed dictator of Louisiana.

Typed in his day as a fascist or an ignorant buffoon, Huey Long was actually a complex man of remarkable intellectual gifts who defies easy classification. Many of his neighbors loved him and reverently recalled the accomplishments of his administration: a splendid network of highways, elimination of the poll tax, expansion of hospital services, and generous appropriations for the public schools. The claims are indisputable. Yet they were realized by an administration which was a cheerful combination of pragmatism and cynicism, persuasion and coercion. The moralists groaned, but the roads were built. "We got the roads in Louisiana," Long said. "In some states they only have the graft."[6]

Long was in his time, and is today, an enigma. Nowhere were the contradictory elements in his character more clearly manifested than in his relations with Louisiana State University. When Warren arrived there in 1934, he found abundant evidence of Long's achievement and of his high-handed tactics. "This is," Long liked to say, "my university."[7] He poured money into college buildings, including the million-dollar Huey P. Long Field House. The enrollment doubled, then doubled again. When the school newspaper dared to criticize him, he suspended it. When Warren and his colleagues founded the *Southern Review* in 1935, the possibility of interference caused them to agree to resign if their editorial prerogatives were challenged. They were not, however, subjected to either political or academic pressure during their tenure as editors.[8]

Huey Long was assassinated in the capitol at Baton Rouge on September 8, 1935, by Dr. Carl Austin Weiss, Jr. Weiss's motives were apparently more personal than political. His father, while head of the state medical association, had fought Long's meddling in faculty affairs of the medical school of Tulane University. Weiss's father-in-law, a state judge, was about to be gerrymandered out of his office, and Long had implied that there was Negro blood in the judge's family. Long's death, like so much else in his career, was melodramatic, and his story has ever since had a magnetic appeal for novelists. Hamilton Basso, in *Sun in Capricorn*, treated the matter superficially and inconclusively. John Dos Passos's *Number One* is indebted to the Long story, as is Sinclair Lewis's *It Can't Happen Here*. In 1946, the same year as *All the King's Men*, Adria Locke Langley published *A Lion Is in the Street*, also about a politician resembling Long.

All the King's Men is not, however, fictional biography. Warren has dissociated himself from the opinions of the early reviewers who rushed forward to accuse him of writing an "apologia" for Huey Long. Warren is explicit on this point: "Willie Stark was not Huey Long. Willie was only himself, whatever that self turned out to be, a shadowy wraith or a blundering human being."[9] Nevertheless, the externals of Long's career closely parallel those of Willie Stark's. Like Huey Long, Willie Stark comes from a section of a southern state (never named in the novel) which suddenly prospers with the coming of sawmills, then relapses into poverty after the fields are denuded. Willie, like his prototype, studies late into the night in a Lincolnesque effort at self-education. He earns his living by peddling from door to door a Fix-It-Yourself kit (Long sold a product called Cottalene). The general outline of Long's political career—his grassroots appeal to the rural districts,

his development of a political machine, his bodyguards, his impeachment, his senatorial and presidential ambitions—provide a framework
for the novel. Stark's legislative programs—the educational system,
highway construction, free medical care, tax reform—are identical
with Long's. Finally, the circumstances of the assassination are remarkably similar. The resemblances, however, are only in externals, for, as
Warren has wisely said, "suggestion does not mean identity, and even
if I had wanted to make Stark a projection of Long, I should not have
known how to go about it."[10]

II All the King's Men and Narrator Jack Burden

In telling the story of the rise and fall of Willie Stark, Warren did
not wish to write a "straight naturalistic novel." He felt the "necessity
for a character of a higher degree of self-consciousness than my politician, a character to serve as a kind of commentator and raisonneur
and chorus. . . . So Jack Burden entered the scene."[11]

The Jack Burden we meet in the opening paragraph of the novel is,
in many ways, the ideal narrator. He is, first of all, an historian with
the historian's devotion to "fact." He is not squeamish about ransacking
the "sad detritus of time" which is the "human past" (205). Moreover,
Jack loves Truth, loves it voraciously, with a precise, judicious, almost
niggling dedication. "It was always that way," he is likely to say, and
then, on second thought, to add, "or like that" (156). He has the historian's sensitivity to the impingement of the past on the present, and
the substance of the novel consists of three projects of historical
research. First, there is the subject of Jack's doctoral dissertation, the
journal of Cass Mastern. Second, there is the project of digging up the
dirt on Judge Montague Irwin. And finally, there is the novel itself:
Jack's reconstruction of his own past and that of Willie Stark.

Jack has another quality which particularly fits him for the role of
historian: an insatiable, compulsive curiosity. He is continually seeking
the elusive moment of illumination, the "dazzle" which will explain all
and justify all. Watching the headlights of his car probing into the
night, he ponders on the "blazing" corridor of light which splits the
dark in front of him but which, no matter what his speed, remains
tantalizingly beyond him. Or crossing the state on a train, Jack sees a
sudden flash of sunlight as a woman comes out of her farmhouse door
and throws a basin of water to the ground. Watching her return to the
house, Jack feels that she must know the answer to a question he cannot
even frame.

At the opening of *All the King's Men,* we not only meet Jack Burden in a characteristic mood, but, as in the opening paragraphs of *Night Rider,* we find in embryo the themes which are developed in the course of the novel. A black, official limousine speeds down the highway, a straight, white, glistening slab with a black line painted down the center. In the car are Governor Willie Stark, his wife Lucy, their son Tom, the governor's chauffeur and bodyguard Sugar Boy, and Jack Burden, all bound for Willie's birthplace, a poultry farm outside Mason City in the northern section of a southern state. Jack Burden, his eyes glued to the road, is speculating nervously on the possibilities for disaster for "two tons of expensive mechanism" hurtling down the highway at eighty miles per hour: " . . . if you don't quit staring at that line and don't take a few deep breaths and slap yourself hard on the back of the neck you'll hypnotize yourself and you'll come to just at the moment when . . . [the automobile] starts the dive" (3).

The opening paragraphs render with Naturalistic detail the surface and texture of the scene, but the richness of language indicates that the scene carries the additional suggestiveness of symbolism with its literal and latent levels of meaning. The highway is raised to the level of the archetypal symbol of each man's progress through life. The predicament of the narrator is summed up by his preoccupation with the line painted down the center of the highway. The line serves as a guide, a source of direction, yet his single-minded devotion to that line has the effect of mesmerizing him so that he is in danger of being destroyed by the very thing which promises his salvation. This effect is reinforced by the onomatopoeia, achieved by the repetition of coordinate elements in the sentences, which suggests the monotonous whine of the tires and the drone of the engine. The machine, in this case an automobile, is a metaphor that embodies the philosophy of mechanistic determinism which Jack Burden, at this point in his own spiritual odyssey, has adopted. And the car that "whips on into the dazzle" accents the miragelike quality of the truth which Jack is perpetually seeking, but which remains elusively beyond his reach.

All the King's Men is essentially the story of Jack Burden, and the significance of the life of Willie Stark is ultimately its significance in the life of Jack Burden. The title of the novel shifts the emphasis from the king to his men, and Jack Burden is Willie's man. Jack denies it. He goes to great pains to dissociate himself from the assorted louts and lackies who surround the governor and relishes those moments when he can look Willie in the eye and threaten to quit. But in a moment of self-betrayal, he humiliates a city policeman and then runs for cover

behind the power of Willie Stark. Although Jack is instantly filled with
self-loathing, the experience provides a measure of his own attraction
to, and corruption by, power. He is caught in a gravitational force
which, at once attracting and repelling, holds him within the orbit of
Willie Stark. At the end, after the fruits of violence and corruption
have been reaped, Jack is still convinced of the governor's stature: "I
must believe that Willie Stark was a great man" (452).

The lives of the two men are inextricably woven together. The structure of the opening chapter emphasizes this interrelationship, for it
divides into two parts, each concerned with the return of a man to the
place of his birth. For Willie Stark it is a return to a poultry farm outside Mason City, an eroded land of swamps and scrub pine, Baptist
fundamentalism, and grinding poverty. For Jack Burden it is a return
to Burden's Landing, a row of handsome estates fronting on the Gulf
where the ancestral portraits look down from richly paneled walls. The
two experiences lead Jack to speculate on a familiar theme in southern
literature—you can't go home again: "The child comes home and the
parents put the hooks in him. . . . It's not love. . . . It is just something
in the blood. It is a kind of blood greed" (39). The reactions to the
experience of homecoming tell much about the two men. On Willie,
the hooks don't snag a thing. "I gotta shove," he says, and shoves. Jack,
on the other hand, returns to find himself caught up in old loyalties
and obligations which pull him back into the depths of the past. These
stirrings of memory lead him to recount, in a series of contrasted
scenes, the rise of Willie Stark from hick idealist to ruthless political
operator. There is Cousin Willie from the country, circa 1922, wearing
Christmas tie and rumpled suit, drinking orange pop and smarting
under the jibes of the state auditor, Tiny Duffy. Then there is Governor
Stark, circa 1936, wearing tailored clothes, drinking Scotch, and anni-
hilating Lieutenant Governor Duffy with a quip.

Despite Jack Burden's efforts to render precisely the form and pressure of his time, the Willie Stark who emerges from the narrative
remains an enigma. Warren has said that behind the novel stand the
"scholarly and benign" figure of William James and the "cold-faced
Florentine," Machiavelli.[12] Certainly Willie is both coldly pragmatic
and engagingly opportunistic. He is more concerned with manipulat-
ing the world as he finds it, in a fatalistic and joyous acceptance of
things as they are, than in plumbing philosophic depths. His philosophy, which he explains on several occasions, is disarmingly simple.
"Badness" is all that exists; one has no choice but to make "goodness"
out of it. Willie's simplistic credo, his cheerful acceptance of the inev-

itability of evil, offends Jack's feeling for nuance and subtlety; and it
fails to satisfy his own curiosity concerning his attraction to Willie.
When Jack queries Willie about their relationship, the answer is cryptic: "You work for me because I'm the way I am and you're the way
you are" (204). Pressed by Jack to explain, Willie can only reply,
"There's something inside you" (278).

Jack's fascination with Willie and his desire to understand that fascination lead him to explore their relationship. Chapters two and three
develop, in a series of intricately plotted flashbacks, the educations of
the two men. The focus is properly kept on Willie Stark. The story
traces the transformation of Cousin Willie, political idealist, into Governor Willie, political realist, and incorporates most of the elements of
the Long legend that Warren has chosen to use.

In the course of the exposition, we learn a good deal indirectly about
Jack Burden. During the years that he is watching Cousin Willie being
transformed into a southern Machiavelli, Jack persists in his own
"brass-bound" idealism. This idealism is the earliest stage in his spiritual autobiography. It is a philosophy, he tells us, he got from a book
in college, but for him it is less a philosophy than a strategy of retreat
and withdrawal. ("The world was full of things I didn't want to know"
[151].) His history is revealed obliquely in tangled memories and sentimental reveries, but the reason for his malaise gradually emerges. He
believes his mother to be a brittle, shallow woman incapable of love.
Her husband, Ellis Burden, lives in a slum and distributes religious
tracts on street corners. Jack can feel only pity for one and contempt
for the other. The woman Jack loves, Anne Stanton, has rejected him
because of the apparent purposelessness of his life.

Jack Burden's lip service to idealism is, therefore, largely a sneering
distrust of speculative thought, of all formal efforts to explain life. But
events, coupled with his inquisitive temperament, force speculation
upon him. Each new discovery, each stage in his intellectual and spiritual development, is announced by a Big Sleep, a complete retreat into
unconsciousness often accompanied by a flight westward, "drowning
in west." The imagery of this process is Freudian in its inspiration and
operates as a motif of spiritual death and rebirth. Although living in an
atmosphere of political corruption, Jack smugly refuses to believe that
he can be contaminated. He shrinks from the awful possibility that he
may discover evil within himself. Only by being reborn through a
realization of the burden of guilt he shares with all men can he be said
to be wholly man.

Jack Burden is a divided man, sick with the "terrible division" of his age. Fragmented himself, he sees the world divided against itself. This division is dramatized by the fact that there are two Jack Burdens, the one who is telling the story and the other to whom the events happened. Such comments as "But that summer from the height of my Olympian wisdom, I seemed to find a great many things funny which now do not appear quite as funny" (338) remind us that time has passed and things are different. The effect is even more emphatically dramatized in the fourth chapter when the point of view shifts radically from the first-person narrator to the third person, and we are introduced to another Jack Burden "of whom the present Jack Burden, *ME*, is a legal, biological, and perhaps even metaphysical continuator" (168). Although the story is apparently told by one person, Warren has actually employed a dual narrator through which the story is refracted. His intricate handling of chronology involves having two and sometimes three levels of time alternately or simultaneously holding the stage, a technique which owes something to Conrad and to Faulkner. The present narrator, moreover, is a conscious artist who withholds information from the reader to kindle suspense and to create anew the shock of discovery. Warren's handling of these points of view, together with his manipulation of chronology, is the great technical triumph of the novel.

Jack Burden's efforts at integration of self are thwarted by his inclination toward abstraction. He generalizes people, including himself, into types. He is the College Boy, the Brass-Bound Idealist, or the Master Mind, behaving and responding in a stereotyped fashion which releases him from the responsibility for his actions. The procession of his mother's husbands includes the Scholarly Attorney, the Tycoon, the Count, and the Young Executive. Adam Stanton, a puzzle to the mature Jack, is understandable as the Friend of His Youth. Even Willie Stark becomes "the Boss," a baffling character in whom Jack "must" believe.

Jack's mind, running as it does to abstraction, tends to polarize terms of thought. He contrasts the urban metropolis of the capital with the remote and rural heartland of Mason City and Burden's Landing: one is the world of public affairs; the other, of private experience. These are correlatives for two spheres of sensibility: one of isolation and alienation and the other of stability and meaning.

In a similar fashion, Jack tends to pair off the main figures in the drama. The friend of his youth, Adam Stanton, he comes to call the "man of idea," and the friend of his maturity, Willie Stark, the "man of fact." Each was doomed to destroy the other, "just as each was doomed to try to use the other and to yearn toward and try to become the other, because each was incomplete with the terrible division of their age" (462). In the same way, Jack contrasts Willie Stark and Tiny Duffy; the two men represent poles in the spectrum of practical politics, and Tiny serves as an alter-ego on whom Willie heaps contempt and insult "because of a blind, inward necessity" (105). Furthermore, Jack sees in Willie a reflection of his own deep-seated division of self. Willie seems always two people: the innocent and idealistic Cousin Willie and the dynamic and masterful governor. Jack categorizes his two "fathers" as temperamental opposites, Ellis Burden the "good, weak father" and Montague Irwin the "evil, strong one." Jack thinks of his two roommates in graduate school in the same terms: one industrious, stupid, unlucky, and alcoholic and the other idle, intelligent, lucky, and alcoholic. Jack's style is informed by this same division, a mixture of the consciously literary and elegant with the earthy and bawdy.

The pressure of events forces Jack to abandon his position as a brass-bound idealist and to embrace a philosophy which, again with his tendency toward abstraction and generalization, he calls "the Great Twitch." Warren has testified to his interest in Naturalistic determinism while at work on the novel,[13] and the Great Twitch is a metaphor for the cluster of ideas associated with that philosophy. For Jack it expresses the mindless, meaningless series of stimuli which provoke an automatic response. Man is but a collection of atoms which spin merrily, or not so merrily. The Great Twitch is the "dream of our age," the dream that all life is but the "dark heave of the blood and the twitch of the nerve" (329). This austere philosophy has its consolations, for it releases the actor from the consequences of his act and makes possible a new "innocence."

The philosophy of the Great Twitch is symbolized in *All the King's Men* by a recurring pattern of machine imagery. This era is, we are told at the beginning of the novel, the "age of the internal combustion engine." Jack's first wife, Lois, he comes to regard as a "sweet-smelling, sweet-breathed machine" (321). The young Willie Stark, dejected and defeated, wearily paces up and down in his hotel "until the machine wore out" (76). The most elaborate treatment of this idea is the prefrontal lobotomy performed by Dr. Adam Stanton on a catatonic schizophrenic (a mental disease which points to the divided nature of modern man). The operation is carried out with a "contraption like a brace and bit" and a "Gigli saw," tools which give access to the "real mechanism" inside. For Jack it is all "high-grade carpenter work," and he is prompted to baptize the patient in the "name of the Great Twitch" (338). The Great Twitch, the "accident of circumstance," fails eventually to satisfy Jack's needs. And he comes to believe Willie Stark's dying words, "It might all have been different, Jack" (425).

In tracing the stages of Jack Burden's philosophic growth, we come finally to the fact that he is, as he so frequently reminds us, a historian; and it is from his meditations on the past that the inner logic of *All the King's Men* emerges. The formulation of Jack's philosophy of history begins with his first journey into the past—his study of the journal of Ellis Burden's maternal uncle, Cass Mastern. Readers acquainted with the Willie Proudfit episode in *Night Rider* and with the "Statement of Ashby Wyndham" in *At Heaven's Gate* will not be surprised when Warren turns suddenly to a story apparently unrelated to Willie Stark. The Cass Mastern episode, Chapter Four of the novel, is a superb evocation of the antebellum South and a bravura piece of imaginative historical reconstruction. The narrative, in contrast to the complex interweaving of episodes in the narrative of Willie Stark, is chronological. The style, in contrast to the flippant and cynical reportorial style of Jack Burden, is coolly objective.

The story deals with two brothers. Gilbert Mastern, confident and self-contained, serves unscathed throughout the Civil War, loses a fortune in defeat, and recoups it during Reconstruction. Cass Mastern, sensitive and brooding, becomes involved in a love affair with the wife of his best friend, Duncan Trice. Learning of the affair, Trice commits suicide; and his wife, Annabella, in a fit of despondency, blames Cass and dismisses him. Filled with remorse, Cass enters the Confederate Army; marches into battle, refusing to bear arms; and, in the fighting outside Atlanta, finds the bullet he is seeking. From these experiences Burden draws a moral about the nature of the world, a moral which is embodied in the central metaphor of the novel:

[Cass] learned that the world is like an enormous spider web and if you touch it, however lightly, at any point, the vibration ripples to the remotest perimeter and the drowsy spider feels the tingle and is drowsy no more but springs out to fling the gossamer coils about you who have touched the web and then inject the black, numbing poison under your hide. It does not matter whether or not you meant to brush the web of things. Your happy foot or your gay wing may have brushed it ever so lightly, but what happens always happens and there is the spider, bearded black and with his great faceted eyes glittering like mirrors in the sun, or like God's eye, and the fangs dripping. (200)

Jack Burden's initial fascination with the story of Cass Mastern stems from the hope that he may come to know himself through his knowledge of another. Certain parallels encourage him in his quest. Like Cass, Jack is a seeker and a dreamer, oblivious to the fact that actions involve responsibility. By an ironic reversal, Jack has behaved "nobly" with Anne Stanton, yet has "by an obscure and necessary logic" driven her into the arms of Willie Stark. He finds it puzzling that his "nobility" has had a consequence as dire in his world as Cass Mastern's sin had had in his. Jack studies Cass Mastern's intimate journal for eighteen months, scrupulously documents the "facts" of his life, but eventually abandons the project in despair. He finds its meaning only when he sees it in the broader perspective provided by his second research project, undertaken this time on orders from Willie Stark: the search for evidence of corruption in the life of Judge Irwin.

Since Judge Irwin had been the idol of Jack's childhood, Jack undertakes the quest largely to disprove Stark's theory that there is evidence of evil in the life of every man. But Jack's last illusion is shattered; the Judge had once accepted a bribe. Confronted by Jack with the evidence, Irwin takes his own life. The aftermath of the suicide uncovers still another sin. Irwin, like Cass Mastern, had committed adultery with the wife of a trusted friend, Ellis Burden. The consequence in each case was the same—three blighted lives. Thus Jack finds yet another parallel between himself and Cass Mastern: both have hounded a man to suicide. Jack had not meant to touch the web, but it had vibrated to the remotest perimeter.

The image of the spider web serves Jack as an explanation for the assassination of Willie Stark. The question arises, who is responsible for Willie's death? Certainly Willie is partly to blame. Jettisoning the philosophy he has taught Jack, that good and evil are inextricable, Willie determines, after the death of his son, to redirect the course of his life and cleanse his administration. With this attempted return to innocence, Willie is swept down in the avalanche he begins. By banishing the corrupt contractor Gummy Larson, Willie offends Tiny Duffy and brings about the collapse of the political machine. In deciding to return to his wife, from whom he is separated, Willie excites the wrath of his mistress, Sadie Burke, who, years before when he had strayed, had prophesied, "I'll kill him" (150). She thinks of herself as the murderess, but it is Tiny Duffy who has informed Adam Stanton that Willie is having an affair with his sister, Anne. And it is Adam who pulls the trigger. Adam's motive, in the best southern tradition of honor and violence, is to avenge the defilement of his sister. Tom Stark, the governor's son, shares in the communal guilt, for his incorrigible behavior, in large part a consequence of his father's indulgence, has inspired Willie to purge himself of evil. Tom, like Jack Burden, cannot be absolved from having caused his father's death. In the widening circle of guilt, Jack sees himself "involved in some monstrous conspiracy."

The cost of making sense out of history has been high, so high in fact that Jack has come to feel that perhaps the only worthwhile knowledge is that which "has cost some blood." But, amid the wreckage of so many lives, he is at last ready to frame his philosophy of history. It is found in its most simplified form in a speech to his mother at the conclusion of the novel: "I tried to tell her how if you could not accept the past and its burden there was no future, for without one there cannot be the other, and how if you could accept the past you might hope for the future, for only out of the past can you make the future" (461). This knowledge has been won from his two excursions into the past. From his study of Cass Mastern's journals, Jack has learned the isolation and alienation of the human condition. "It is a human defect," Cass had written, "to try to know oneself by the self of another. One can only know oneself in God and in His great eye" (184). Armed with this knowledge, Jack is ready to accept the insight of Ellis Burden that the separation of man from man is but the imperfect reflection of the separation of man from God:

Separateness is identity and the only way for God to create, truly create, man was to make him separate from God Himself, and to be separate from God is to be sinful. The creation of evil is therefore the index of God's glory and His power. That had to be so that the creation of good might be the index of man's glory and power. But by God's help. (462–63)

Jack thus comes to realize the paradox of identity: that knowledge of self consists in a recognition not only of man's isolation but also of the burden of sin that binds all men. Only through acceptance of this dilemma can the split sensibility of modern man hope to achieve integration of self—or, in terms of the novel's title, to put Humpty Dumpty together again. Such spiritual wholeness as is possible for man lies in his capacity for love.[14] "If you loved," Jack says, "and were loved perfectly, then there wouldn't be any difference between the two you's. . . . They would coincide perfectly . . . as when a stereoscope gets the twin images on the card into perfect adjustment" (299). This theme is further reinforced by the epigraph of the novel taken from Dante:

"Not by the malediction of bishop or priest is Eternal Love so lost, that it cannot return again, *as long as hope hath still a speck of green.*" Salvation lies in a realm of spirit beyond all the king's horses and all the king's men of this world.

Jack's newfound knowledge is meaningless, however, if it is isolated from the flux of history and raised to a chilly pinnacle of abstraction. The fullness of life can be realized only in the concreteness of the present moment. Jack's immersion in the past has shown him that "meaning is never in the event but in the motion through event" (287). The present moment is the point in time in which the past is made manifest and the future determined. Life is motion, a process not of being but of becoming. Thus a matured and chastened Jack Burden can enter, with Anne Stanton, "the convulsion of the world, out of history into history and the awful responsibility of Time" (464).

All the King's Men is one of those rare books that appeal equally to the literary intelligentsia and to the so-called common readers. It shows every sign of possessing remarkable staying power, for it continues to generate intellectual excitement and passionate identification. Hollywood paid it the compliment of an adaptation, and although lacking the thematic richness of the novel, the film was successful enough to win an Academy Award.

III   All the King's Men: *The Dramatic Version*

The translation of *All the King's Men* to the screen confirmed Warren's original impulse that the theme lent itself to dramatic treatment. He has, in fact, repeatedly returned to his material to revise it for the stage. The original conception, the verse drama "Proud Flesh," has never been published, although it was produced in April 1946 at the University of Minnesota where Warren was teaching. Patterned loosely on Greek tragedy, "Proud Flesh" focuses on a southern politician of heroic mold, Willie Talos, who falls because of the fatal flaw of hubris. Warren employed a chorus of surgeons who comment on the action, and Jack Burden appears only fleetingly in the closing moments of the play to evoke in the assassin, Keith Amos, the poignant memory of the innocence of their childhood. A second version of the drama, also unpublished, was presented in 1947 by the Dramatic Workshop of the New School for Social Research under the title "All the King's Men." This time Warren substituted a professor of science for the chorus and rewrote and amplified the plot to bring it into closer harmony with the action of the novel.[15] The result was a crowded stage and a complicated narrative line which led Wolcott Gibbs to remark in the *New Yorker* that Warren had "exercised almost no selection, and the unnecessary complex of stories on the stage might easily be quite incomprehensible to anyone who hadn't read the book."[16] Warren may have agreed with this criticism, for in the third version of the play, produced off-Broadway in October 1959 and published the following year as *All the King's Men: A Play,* Warren greatly simplified the action, eliminated the choric commentary, and reduced the number of scenes from twenty-four to a prologue and three acts. But whatever the play's merits as theater, it will inevitably be judged against the novel, and that is stiff competition indeed. In the play, Warren employed a character, the "Professor," who, paired with Jack Burden, generates in some measure the tension achieved through the novel's use of a dual narrator. And the play naturally gains impact from the simplicity of plot and economy of action.

But Warren himself points to the central difficulty of the play in his essay on Joseph Conrad's novel *Nostromo.* Conrad, Warren tells us, wished "to arrive at his meanings immediately, through the sensuous renderings of passionate experience, and not merely to define meanings in abstraction, as didacticism or moralizing."[17] Whereas the meanings of the novel emerge organically from the texture of the experience, the meanings of the drama seem imposed upon the action from without. The characters make their points with a shrill insistence that renders them but shadowy projections of their counterparts in the novel. What Warren achieved in his novel is, to use one of his own favorite words, *inwardness. All the King's Men* is a novel which needs, indeed demands, repeated readings to reveal its richly convolved meanings. In *Night Rider* and *At Heaven's Gate* Warren had demonstrated that he could create incident and character and that he was possessed of a talent which, in its extravagance and gusto, was reminiscent of the Elizabethans. With the publication of *All the King's Men,* it became apparent that his gifts had matured through a rigorous and disciplined apprenticeship to his art. From the Naturalists he had learned the necessity not only of documenting his imaginative world, but also of conceiving it in terms of a philosophic order. From the Symbolists he had learned a technique of endowing his creation with the suggestiveness and depth of human experience. In the fusion of these two traditions Warren has given us in *All the King's Men* a version of the modern world, startling in its freshness and terrifying in its accuracy.

IV *Warren and Coleridge's* The Ancient Mariner

Warren was engaged in writing *All the King's Men* from the spring of 1943 until the fall of 1945, but his work was frequently interrupted, first by his teaching responsibilities at the University of Minnesota and then, in 1944, by his appointment to the post of Consultant in Poetry at the Library of Congress. Moreover, in keeping with his enormous capacity for work, Warren had undertaken simultaneously with the writing of the novel a critical analysis of Coleridge's *The Ancient Mariner* which appeared in 1946 as the foreword to an edition of the poem.

Warren's magisterial explication of the poem is buttressed by an erudite and searching commentary on Coleridge's philosophic and critical theories. Addressing himself to the critics who have found the poem incoherent, Warren argues for a symbolic reading in terms of a primary theme of the sacramental vision, or the "One Life," and a secondary theme of the imagination, a term Warren asks us to define in the special sense used by Coleridge in his philosophic discourse ("the living power and prime agent of all human perception").

In Warren's reading, the mariner's shooting of the albatross is a symbolic representation of Original Sin, a manifestation of the inscrutable perversity of man's will. The act is devoid of motivation, thus constituting a reenactment of the Fall. The other mariners are implicated in the crime, for they too have violated the sacramental nature of the universe by treating it with indifference. Although the bird is "pious" and of "good omen," the mariners condone the act on practical grounds, "by making man's convenience the measure of his acts." "The Mariner," Warren writes, "shoots the bird; suffers various pains, the greatest of which is loneliness and spiritual anguish; upon recognizing the beauty of the foul sea snakes experiences a gush of love for them and is able to pray; is returned miraculously to his home port, where he discovers the joy of human communion in God, and utters the moral, 'He prayeth best who loveth best, etc.' We arrive at the notion of universal charity . . . the sense of the 'One Life' in which all creation participates."[18] Thus the fable, in Warren's opinion, dramatizes an essentially Christian statement of sin, punishment, repentance, and redemption.

Since Warren was explicating *The Ancient Mariner* at the same time that he was writing *All the King's Men*, it is tempting to speculate on the motives that drew him to Coleridge's poem while he was exploring the themes which form the intellectual structure of the novel. Certainly there are suggestive parallels between the two works. Both are examples of the archetypal story of Rebirth or the Night Journey, and in *All the King's Men* this fable is emphasized by an explicit pattern of imagery. The plight of Jack Burden, and that of Cass Mastern, resembles that of the mariner—"loneliness and spiritual anguish." Also, both Jack and Cass, having achieved a kind of redemption, feel a compulsion to tell their story. The parallel with *The Ancient Mariner* is further enhanced by the marine and nautical imagery which recurs like a leitmotif throughout the novel. And finally, a Coleridgean comment on the will, as quoted by Warren in his essay, could stand as the epigraph to *All the King's Men:* "But in its utmost abstraction and consequent state of reprobation, the will becomes Satanic pride and rebellious self-idolatry in the relations of the spirit to itself, and remorseless despotism relatively to others . . . by the fearful resolve to find in itself alone the one absolute motive of action."[19]

V   *"Blackberry Winter" and Other Short Stories*

Released suddenly from the concentrated work necessary to complete *All the King's Men* and the critical essay on *The Ancient Mariner*, Warren in the spring of 1946 found himself in a retrospective mood. Living in the heart of Minneapolis, a northern city where snow was still falling in May, he was, as he said, "indulging nostalgia" in recalling the coming of spring in his native Kentucky and Tennessee. The chain of association sparked by those memories led to a short story, "Blackberry Winter," which was published in 1946.

The action of the story is simply the events of one morning in the life of a nine-year-old boy who lives on a tobacco farm in rural Tennessee. The surface of each scene is rendered with the pristine freshness it would have for the mind of a sensitive and observant child. The June morning dawns cold and damp, a season called blackberry winter because of its unnatural and unpleasant retrogression from the warmth of spring. The boy, Seth, resents his mother's insistence that he wear shoes that spring morning, for the day promises the excitement of exploration about the farm. A storm the night before, a "gully washer," has flooded the creek, washing out crops and spreading destruction over the countryside.

Each of the apparently trivial details of the boy's excursion about the neighborhood builds toward the moment of illumination. Seth examines the "stringy and limp" bodies of drowned chicks whose eyes have "that bluish membrane over them which makes you think of a very old man who is sick about to die." With a crowd of neighbors, the boy watches a dead cow floating down the creek and listens uncomprehendingly to a veteran of Forrest's cavalry ruminate on human privation. When he goes to the usually immaculate cabin of two Negroes, Dellie and Jebb, to play with their son, Little Jebb, Seth feels some unformulated stirrings of disenchantment when he finds that the storm has washed trash and filth out from under the cabin. The shock of sudden violence intrudes when Dellie, suffering from "woman mizry," cruelly slaps Little Jebb for playing too noisily. When Seth asks Old Jebb for an explanation of Dellie's unaccustomed ill temper, he replies, "Hit is the change of life and time." The tone of foreboding is enhanced when Old Jebb predicts that "this-here old yearth is tahrd . . . and ain't gonna perduce."

These apparently random incidents are brought suddenly and sharply into focus by Seth's experience with a tramp, a knife-wielding and worthless drifter apparently cast up, like refuse, by the storm. The inquisitive child trails him from the farm, trying to draw him into conversation. Abruptly the tramp turns on him and snarls, "You don't stop following me and I cut yore throat, you little son-of-a-bitch." "But I did follow him," the narrator adds, "all the years."

In the span of a single morning, the child has experienced his own blackberry winter. He has been thrust suddenly and violently from the warmth of his childish innocence to the chill knowledge of the "jags and injustices" of an adult world. Each of the events of the day is a correlative of loss and change, and each is expressed through a series of ironic contrasts: the benevolence and malevolence of nature, the timeless world of the child and the time-obsessed world of the adult, the rooted and intimately familiar farm and the rootless and alien city. Seth tells the story, but what we hear is the memory of that June morning recounted thirty-five years after the event. The man is looking backward on the boy he once was, recalling objectively his childhood bewilderment. The events of the day had puzzled the child, but the man, remembering the experience, is not puzzled. Rather he now sees the experience as a paradigm of a problem he has carried into adulthood. He has come to terms with the problem—it is one mark of his maturity—but it is a problem that is never finally resolved. It is the imaginative awareness of what Warren has called, in speaking of "Blackberry Winter," the "human communion."[20] The narrator of the story recognizes that the brotherhood of man must embrace even the contemptible, cowardly, and defeated tramp of the story; and he grasps the sense of responsibility that such a recognition entails.

"Blackberry Winter" is the finest among the fourteen short stories Warren collected in 1948 under the title *The Circus in the Attic*. The contents of the book go back to 1930 with the inclusion of "Prime Leaf," and several of the stories date from the period of the *Southern Review*. The only story that approaches "Blackberry Winter" in its exercise of creative control over its material is "The Patented Gate and the Mean Hamburger." The resemblances between the two stories may be traced to the fact that both were written in the spring of 1946 when thoughts of his southern boyhood were much in Warren's mind.

"The Patented Gate and the Mean Hamburger" develops quietly and slowly, seeming at first scarcely a story at all. It describes a type of Tennessee farmer—red-necked, gaunt-faced, tight-lipped—from whom the central character, Jeff York, differs only in his modest prosperity. The symbol of his years of sweat and deprivation is a patented gate, an elaborate contraption of crossbars and braces operated mechanically, which opens to his dirt farm. Stroke by stroke, a portrait is built up of the people who inhabit the nearby town where Jeff, his wife, and their children spend each Saturday afternoon: the citified and contemptuous owner of a diner, Slick Hardin; the snickering townsfolk sitting at his counter munching their hamburgers; the condescending bank president, Todd Sullivan. Forced by his wife to sell his farm and buy Slick Hardin's diner, Jeff York stoically establishes her in town. Then, without a word, he walks out to his farm and hangs himself from the patented gate. The story is narrated by an anonymous spokesman for the town, and from the opening sentence ("You have seen him a thousand times") we are made gradually aware that the members of the community, despising as they do hick dumbness, are inescapably involved in the suicide of Jeff York.

The story from which the collection takes its title, "The Circus in the Attic," returns to the Bardsville of *Night Rider*, ranging backward to the founding of the village and its part in the Civil War and forward to the slum-ridden factory town of the present. The plot chronicles the life of Bolton Loveheart, a mother-dominated and bloodless town aristocrat who finds meaning in his later years by idealizing his stepson, a Medal of Honor hero of World War II. Certain scenes in the story are vintage Warren: the evocation of the town's history, the death of Bolton's mother, the hilarious recounting of a Yankee raid by the town derelict. A rambling and diffuse story, it seems more a synopsis of a Warren novel than a fully realized short story.

"The Circus in the Attic," in fact, points to a weakness in many of the stories in this collection. The prodigality of Warren's talent, his gift for sustained narrative and invention, seems cramped within the confines of the short story. He has written nothing in the form since 1946, and in an autobiographical note on the writing of "Blackberry Winter," he bade farewell to the genre.[21] How far the form of the short story was from satisfying his artistic needs may be surmised by the fact that, while collecting his short stories in 1948, he was hard at work on his longest and most complex novel, *World Enough and Time*, which appeared in the spring of 1950.

CHAPTER 5

The Distance of the Past

I   World Enough and Time

IN *World Enough and Time* the full-dress documentation of the past in the manner of the Cass Mastern episode in *All the King's Men* is expanded to an entire novel. Following as it did the critical and popular success of *All the King's Men, World Enough and Time* appears, in the Warren canon, to be an attempt at a magnum opus. In writing this novel Robert Penn Warren perhaps intended—as he said Joseph Conrad intended in *Nostromo*—"to create a great, massive, multiphase symbol that would render his total vision of the world, his sense of individual destiny, his sense of man's place in nature, his sense of history and society."[1]

Despite the radical shift to a remote time and place, *World Enough and Time* is an elaboration and extension of themes already dealt with in *All the King's Men*. The plot concerns the murder by Jeremiah Beaumont of a politican and lawyer, Colonel Cassius Fort. In Fort, as in Willie Stark, good and evil are inextricably mixed. The narrator of the novel asks: "If Fort did good, could that wipe out his evil?" (132). "He was good," another character adds, "but his good is mixed up with his foulness" (434). Again like Stark, Fort is destroyed by the southern tradition of personal honor and violence. The responsibility for Fort's death spreads throughout *World Enough and Time* just as the responsibility for Stark's death spreads throughout *All the King's Men*, staining each of the major characters. In the later novel Warren has concentrated on the "innocent" idealist, Jeremiah Beaumont, who, like Adam Stanton, does the deed and, in so doing, is used by a world he does not understand. Jeremiah bears a relationship to Jack Burden as well: like Jack, he must tell his story and, in the telling, try to reconcile the worlds of fact and of idea.

Warren's inspiration for the novel was a pamphlet which Katherine Anne Porter showed him in 1944 when both were fellows at the

Library of Congress. "I read it in five minutes," Warren said, "but I was six years making the book."[2] Published in Bloomfield, Kentucky, in 1826, and entitled *The Confession of Jereboam O. Beauchamp*, the pamphlet is the chief document in an ancient and celebrated murder-seduction story—the Sharp-Beauchamp case—which has held a continuing fascination for American writers. In the 1830s it formed the basis of plays by Edgar Allan Poe, Thomas Holly Chivers, and Charlotte Barnes. Charles Fenno Hoffman incorporated some of the elements of the tale into his romance *Greyslaer*, and William Gilmore Simms stayed closer to the facts as known in *Charlemont* and in its sequel, *Beauchampe*.

The original story is compounded of high tragedy and farce comedy, innocence and corruption, honesty and duplicity. A young attorney, Jereboam O. Beauchamp, heard the story of the seduction and betrayal of Ann Cook by the solicitor-general of Kentucky, Colonel Solomon P. Sharp. Beauchamp impetuously sought her out and proposed marriage, but she would consent only on condition that he vow to murder Sharp. Although Beauchamp was an acquaintance of Sharp and easily provoked a quarrel, Sharp repeatedly refused to accept a challenge. The lovers then conspired together to murder Sharp, and Jereboam stabbed him to death on the night of November 6, 1825. Beauchamp was arrested and pleaded not guilty, but he was convicted after a trial which was marked by corruption on both sides. Although the grand jury had released Ann, she joined Jereboam in his cell where they awaited the day of execution by composing prayers and poems, singing hymns, and making love. When the governor refused a plea for pardon, they attempted to commit suicide by taking laudanum the night before the execution was to take place. When this failed, Jereboam stabbed Ann to death and wounded himself; but he lived long enough to be hanged the following day.

The story has all the trappings of unabashed melodrama—innocence violated, villainy triumphant, honor avenged—and Warren has remained remarkably faithful to both the letter and the spirit of his sources. Yet it is precisely because of his gaudy materials that Warren has chosen to remove us two steps from the action through his handling of the point of view. The novel begins:

I can show you what is left. After the pride, passion, agony, and bemused aspiration, what is left is in our hands. . . . Here is the manuscript he himself

wrote, day after day, as he waited in his cell, telling his story. . . . To whom
was he writing, rising from his mire or leaning from his flame to tell his story?
The answer is easy. He was writing to us.

At once we are introduced to the narrator-historian, the "I" of the
story, who has diligently searched out and now displays, often with the
professional flourish of the guild historian, the assembled documents.
He continually interjects himself to parade the sources, sift the evidence, and analyze the motives. He is forever at the reader's elbow,
gently pointing the path through a maze of contradictory testimony,
hinting at the need for both detachment and sympathy, reminding him
of the contemporary relevance of the events. The code duello, for
example, may seem to the sophisticate a quaint and rather fatuous contest between "dunces," but the narrator muses on its modern equivalent: "We do not stand up at dawn, but we lie in a scooped-out hole in
a tropical jungle and rot in the rain and wait for the steel pellet whipping through the fronds. . . . we ride a snarling motor into the veil of
flak" (128).

Such a technique at first seems a flagrant violation of tone. Warren
knew he was sacrificing immediacy, the illusion of entering a place
remote in time and temper. His method could easily stultify the narrative, as it stultifies so much contemporary historical writing. But the
aesthetic distance Warren gains is actually a way of framing his materials and of giving verisimilitude to events which contain a large element of the absurd. The narrator-historian also supplies an ironic corrective to any hint of antiquarian condescension, "the sad and
contemptuous distance with which we now regard . . . an attic trunk"
(52).

The chief document on which the narrator-historian can draw is the
manuscript journal of Jeremiah Beaumont, written in his jail cell while
he was awaiting execution for the murder of Colonel Fort. The journal
is not a diary, a day-by-day account of the experience as it happened,
but a recollection of the events and a meditation on their significance.
Some readers will not find the overwrought and turgid style of the
journal to their taste, but it is completely in character with its author.
For Jeremiah, his story is heroic drama, full of "noble gestures and
swelling periods, serious as blood" (5). The drama metaphor, occasionally couched in allegorical terms, is sustained throughout the journal;
and, the narrator suggests, it was perhaps a drama Jeremiah "had to
prepare in order to live at all, or in order, living, to be human" (5).

Jeremiah's romantic view of life, a view of "high sentiment and beauty," a muddled mixture formed from his reading of Plato and Byron, cannot stand the test of exposure to the realities of his world:

So after the fine speeches and the tragic stance, the grand exit was muffed. The actors trip on their ceremonial robes, even at the threshold of greatness, and come tumbling down in a smashing pratt-fall, amid hoots and howls from the house, and the house gets its money's worth. . . . It knows where reality abides: in the femur cracked and the buttocks black and blue. (442)

The characters had cast themselves in roles which they were ill-suited to play. They had failed to see that their vision of their destiny was subject to the whim and caprice of others, each of whom was intent on his own private drama.

Jeremiah's failure is his inability to prepare his drama for the two "worlds" with which he must deal. There is the "secret world," subjective, private, ideal; and there is the public world of events, of history, of law and justice. In the Conrad essay already quoted, Warren has said, "Man is precariously balanced in his humanity between the black inward abyss of himself and the black outward abyss of nature."[3] Jeremiah Beaumont is poised just at this point.

Jeremiah is yet another Warren character seeking self-knowledge, hoping to find his identity through the exploration of his private world. "Oh, what am I?" he asks (295), echoing Sue Murdock in *At Heaven's Gate*. And like Jerry Calhoun and Jack Burden, he repeats his name in astonishment, trying to find some connection between the mysterious syllables and his identity. "I am Jeremiah Beaumont, I am Jeremiah Beaumont. But I marveled even at the sound of my name" (393).

The possibility for identity lies in knowledge—of the self and of the world. Jeremiah's search leads him, like Jerry Calhoun, to wish for the death of a parent that he might be released to enjoy worldly success. His search leads him to betray the teacher of his youth, Dr. Leicester Burnham, and the benefactor of his young manhood, Colonel Cassius Fort. Jeremiah drives to suicide the woman he would avenge, Rachel Jordan. And ultimately he finds that "the crime for which I seek expiation is never lost. . . . It is the crime of self, the crime of life. The crime is I" (504–505).

Jeremiah's path to this conclusion Warren gives us with an abundance of detail and commentary which is initially absorbing but eventually tedious. The youth of Jeremiah is portrayed against a background of frontier Kentucky during the early nineteenth century. He is a stiff-necked, aloof young man whose natural shyness preserves his innocence in a society both coarse and brutal. He prefers *Pilgrim's Progress* and Franklin's *Autobiography* to the "brightness of the moment and the tickle of the flesh" (45). His bookish tastes encourage in him a fatal tendency to "cast a passion over the commonness of things" (10). His youthful idealism causes him to reject outright the estate of his maternal grandfather, Morton Marcher, when the offer is made on the condition that he take the old man's name. Identity is not that simple.

Jeremiah undergoes a religious conversion in the best frontier-revival fashion, but his exaltation in his new found grace leads him to a frenzied, brutal copulation with a hag lurking on the edges of a clearing. The experience has its analogue in a youthful memory of an illustration from the *Book of Martyrs*, "the picture of a young woman tied cruelly to a post 'so that the bonds seemed to crush her sweet flesh and her face lifted up while the flames rose about her'" (11). Staring at the picture, he is torn between a desire to rescue her from the flames and a desire to light the fire himself. The picture becomes a kind of paradigm of his relationship with Rachel Jordan and of his meditations on the "paradox and doubleness of life" (114).

Having watched his father die "in the bitterness of worldly failure," Jeremiah determines to carve out a better world for himself. The favorite of his schoolmaster, Dr. Burnham, Jeremiah obtains through him the offer of a place in the law office of Colonel Cassius Fort. When the death of his mother releases him from a filial obligation, he comes under the influence of Fort who is "like a father" to him. The relationship of Jeremiah Beaumont and Cassius Fort (like that of Percy Munn and Senator Tolliver, Jerry Calhoun and Bogan Murdock, Jack Burden and Willie Stark) is one in which an older man, paternal and self-assured, takes as an apprentice a callow but promising youth. Warren parallels the growth of friendship between the two men with the growth of intimacy between Fort and Rachel Jordan. She, too, has recently lost her father and has fallen easily under Fort's spell. There follows the development of confidence in Fort, his seduction of Rachel, and Jeremiah's consequent disillusionment.

Inflamed by a Byronic sense of chivalry, Jeremiah lays siege to Rachel's castle ("the princess chained and enchanted"), forces her to tell him of her seduction and the loss of her stillborn child and wrings from her the command, "Kill Fort!" To Rachel, Jeremiah vows, "We will make what world we will" (79). He longs to commit what he calls the "gratuitous act," the act outside the motives of the world; for, in so doing, he can define himself. Fort becomes "an abstaction." To kill him is to commit "the perfect act, outside the world, pure and untarnished . . . the perfect justice self-defining and since defining self, defining all else" (181).

Fort refuses Jeremiah's challenge, even when threatened with horsewhipping in the streets. He flees Frankfort where Jeremiah has sought him out, then finds business which keeps him in the East for months. While he is away, the death of Rachel's mother opens the way for Jeremiah and Rachel to marry at once. With Fort out of sight and out of mind, Jeremiah turns to the cultivation of his wife's farm. As he constructs the world he had promised her, it brings them, out of fortuitous circumstance, happiness.

In talking of the novel, Warren has said: "I began to think of the political struggle of the time as a kind of mirror I could hold up to the personal story."[4] So with Fort in the wings, Warren shifts the political turmoils of Kentucky to stage center. The struggle is an economic one, an effort on the part of the New Court party to ease the plight of debtors even at the risk of subverting both courts and constitution. The Old Court party is dedicated to sanctity of contract and preservation of the Constitution. The dilemma is an ancient one: is the law manipulative, a pragmatic servant to man's needs ("Where is the voice of Justice but in the belly?"), or is the law a set of enduring, transcendent principles ("Where was the voice of Justice but in the heart?") It is the theme stated in the epigraph to the novel taken from Spenser's *Faerie Queen*: "When Justice was not for most meed outhyred, / But simple Truth did rayne, and was of all admyred."

Although Jeremiah's opinions on the political question are characteristically divided, he is drawn into the campaign on the side of the New Court by a friend, Wilkie Barron, whose surname suggests both his spiritual emptiness and his lordly mastery of his world. The occasion of Jeremiah's entry into politics is an election-day riot in which Old Court partisans attempt to prevent Barron's political associate, Percival Skrogg, from voting. Skrogg is gaunt, tubercular, fanatical, indifferent to the flesh, and dispassionately devoted to the "idea"—in this case, the New Court. (The narrator underlines the contemporary parallel by pausing to remind us that such doctrinaire liberals are "the glory and the horror of our time.") Seeing Skrogg abused by superior force, Jeremiah leaps quixotically to his defense, an action as uncalculated and selfless as his defense of Rachel Jordan.

Skrogg and Barron are projections of the two worlds Jeremiah would reconcile. They are, respectively, the man of idea and the man of fact, emblems of the "terrible division" delineated in *All the King's Men*. Where Skrogg is unworldly, Wilkie comes of a race possessing "total confidence in the world." Together they can seize and mold their world, making Jeremiah their tool; isolated, each is a doomed man. Skrogg discovers that the idea is not enough—at his death he is found to have made his concession to the terrors of the world. Despite his apparent fearlessness, he wore beneath his threadbare shirt a vest of chain mail. "At some point," the narrator remarks, "he had discovered that he was part of the world, after all, and that the pitiful body he wore was part of himself and precious. More precious than any idea" (94). Wilkie discovers that the world is not enough—"One morning he stepped into his bath . . . and shot himself tidily through the heart, without a single spatter of blood on the floor. Nobody knew why he did it" (509).

Skrogg and Barron draw Jeremiah into the campaign and into the public world of politics. He runs for the state legislature on a New Court platform. In a nearby county, Colonel Fort is running on the opposing ticket. When the story of Fort's seduction of Rachel is introduced into the campaign, the memory of Jeremiah's vow is forced upon him. His efforts to withdraw from life, to purify his idea in the flame of privacy ("the bright, secret center of life") fail abysmally. The narrator traces his efforts to enter into a larger world, the dawning upon him of the purpose that "you had to show the world in the world's way":

Because the world had seemed nothing, he had lived in the way of the world, feeling safe because he held the idea, pure, complete, abstract, and self-fulfilling. He had thought that he was redeemed by the idea, that sooner or later the idea would redeem the world.

But now he knew: the world must redeem the idea. (228)

And so he radically changes his strategy: "I would submit the idea to the way of the world" (233).

Persuading himself that to kill Fort publicly would be but to indulge his vanity, Jeremiah prepares an elaborate plot and, under cover of darkness, murders Fort in Frankfort. Jeremiah returns triumphant to Rachel. Brought back to Frankfort for trial, he is defended by Madison of New Court and Hawgood of Old Court, two lawyers drawn with an almost allegorical symmetry: "they stood together, the heavy-fleshed, full-blooded seasoned campaigner, and the Platonic student with the thin, sharp, asymmetrical face" (410). The trial becomes a political contest in which Jeremiah, who would have spurned the world, is swept up by its inexorable forces. He is caught up in a tangled web of truth and half-truth, lie and counterlie. Witnesses are suborned and, in turn, betray their suborners. The scales are tipped against him when Wilkie Barron, fearing the crime will be given a political interpretation and destroy the New Court party, testifies to the motive of personal vengeance. All appeals fail, as does the suicide pact of Rachel and Jeremiah.

At this point in the narrative Warren departs from his sources in the Kentucky Tragedy and has Jeremiah enter on a third stage in his search for identity. Wilkie Barron concocts an escape plan, and Rachel and Jeremiah flee westward to merge into the forests beyond the frontier. Here begins the weirdest tale Warren has given us. It is the story of La Grand' Bosse, a river pirate of almost mythical proportions, who has created by sheer animal force and cunning a community in the heart of the wilderness. The structure of *World Enough and Time* here parallels the two novels that preceded it. In *At Heaven's Gate* Warren had depicted two "worlds," the public world of Bogan Murdock and the private world of Slim Sarrett, only to throw them both into relief by the delineation of still a third world, that of Ashby Wyndham. In *All the King's Men* the two spheres of action of the novel are put into perspective when seen in contrast with the story of Cass Mastern. By turning to the world of La Grand' Bosse in *World Enough and Time*, Warren gains a similar effect.

For Jeremiah, the journey westward is a flight out of time and into nature; he determines "to deny the idea and its loneliness and embrace the world as all" (505). What is left is a mindless and furious descent into the mire of bestiality. Rachel's mind breaks under the strain, and she commits suicide by stabbing herself in the breast, a symbolic reenactment of Fort's murder and a gesture of expiation for her guilt. Jeremiah, diseased and despairing, intends finally to return to Frankfort to give himself up, but he is denied even that satisfaction. He is murdered on the trail by an accomplice in the plot against him who now seeks the reward for his capture.

Such, in broad outline, is the fable, but, as Warren has said, fable is but "symbol for exfoliating theme."[5] The theme of *World Enough and Time* is articulated through the interpenetration of the two worlds of the novel: one, of external action; the other, of private experience. The meaning is manifested in the novel by another antithesis—the clearing and the forest. At the center of the novel is the order man has managed to wrest from chaos, the small clearing of the frontiersman. On the periphery is the encroaching forest, the implacable and lawless forces which threaten on all sides. Clearing and forest are symbols for the inner division of self:

The two worlds impinged, overlay and lapped, blurred and absorbed, twisted together and dissolved like mist. . . . It was a nightmare in which the two worlds, the secret and the public, merged and overlapped and intertwined, their happy doubleness betrayed, betraying him. When they merged and their sharp distinction was lost, you were lost, too. (333–35)

Man's best effort must be to try to reconcile these two aspects of his nature. He is groping toward knowledge of both worlds in order to bring them into harmony; and, since the process is an organic one, it is doomed by the nature of things to incompleteness. For to realize complete fulfillment would be nonbeing or death. Singularly enough, it is the victim, Colonel Cassius Fort, who most firmly grasps this insight. Writing to Rachel in extenuation of his conduct, he describes the dichotomy: "I betrayed you and betrayed others who trusted me, compounding betrayal by betrayal, and for those months I lived in a dream outside the hard world and its duties. Then I came back into the world, and hope to do my duty still, whatever it may be and bear with fortitude the ills and losses" (147).

Finally, man has no choice but to endure, to attempt to create a world he can never fully understand. As the narrator observes, "Jeremiah Beaumont had to create his world or be the victim of a world he did not create." He is, however, both creator *and* victim, victim of the world he did create. Even if Jeremiah could gain the knowledge he seeks from a repudiation of the world, there exists the final paradox that his knowledge must be placed "in the context of the world that it repudiated." As the speaker makes plain in Andrew Marvell's "To His Coy Mistress," there is not world enough and time; man must seize on the present moment and wrest from it what significance he can. Such a conclusion veers close to nihilism, but while the speaker in the poem faces this bleak prospect with gaiety and wit, the narrator of the novel speaks in stark and somber tone. The single possibility of affirmation in the novel is voiced by Jeremiah's jailer, Munn Short. Like Willie

Proudfit in *Night Rider*, Munn Short had traveled to the West and, in a series of adventures on the trail, had experienced a spiritual death and rebirth, achieving something akin to the sacramental vision of life. But Munn Short's affirmation makes no impression on Jeremiah Beaumont. Nor is it singled out by the narrator for special emphasis. At the end of *World Enough and Time*, he merely repeats Jeremiah's own final question: "Was all for nought?"

As a final gloss on the novel, we have Warren's comment on Joseph Conrad: "Wisdom, then, is the recognition of man's condition, . . . living with the ever renewing dilemma of idea as opposed to nature, morality to action, justice to material interests. . . . Man must make his life somehow in the dialectical process of these terms, and in so far as he is to achieve redemption he must do so through an awareness of his condition that identifies him with the general human communion, not in abstraction, not in mere doctrine, but immediately. The victory is never won, the redemption must be continually re-earned."[6]

II Brother to Dragons

In 1944, the same year that Katherine Anne Porter had shown him *The Confession of Jereboam O. Beauchamp*, Warren was investigating another sensational episode in nineteenth-century Kentucky history—the brutal ax-murder of a Negro slave by Lilburn Lewis, the nephew of Thomas Jefferson. Having heard a folk version of the tale during his boyhood, Warren, from the files of newspapers and the Abolition literature in the Library of Congress and from Kentucky courthouse records, gradually pieced together the facts of the episode. The story is, as he said, a "shocker."[7]

During the first decade of the nineteenth century, Thomas Jefferson's brother-in-law, Dr. Charles Lewis, moved from his tidewater Virginia home with his wife, their two sons, and a number of slaves to western Kentucky. There on a bluff overlooking the confluence of the Ohio and Cumberland rivers, he built an elaborate house, "Rocky Hill." When his wife, Lucy, died soon after the move, Dr. Lewis returned to Virginia, leaving his sons, Lilburn and Isham, to manage Rocky Hill. On the night of December 15, 1811, having first assembled his slaves in the meathouse to witness what he was going to do, Lilburn butchered a slave named George for the trivial offense of breaking a favorite pitcher of Lucy Lewis. On the same December night as the murder, the first of a series of earthquakes shook the Mississippi Valley, and for years afterwards God-fearing people pointed to the coincidence as an instance of Divine displeasure.

News of the crime soon leaked out, and the two brothers were arrested and indicted for murder. While at liberty awaiting trial, they made a pact to shoot each other at their mother's grave. For some reason unknown to history, their plans went awry. Lilburn was killed at the grave edge, but Isham escaped into the wilderness. Although he was apprehended, tried, and sentenced to hang for the murder of Lilburn, Isham somehow contrived his escape and, three years later, was reported killed at the Battle of New Orleans, one of the two Americans lost at that engagement. In 1953 Warren published his version of the story under the title *Brother to Dragons: A Tale in Verse and Voices*.

The tale contained a number of elements calculated to attract Warren: a basis in historical fact, a violent murder, a tangled skein of motivation, and an episode obscured by the mists of time. The crime was bloody and bizarre, but its very monstrousness provided an opportunity for the clearest statement of what, in retrospect, emerges as *the* Warren theme: "All life lifts and longs toward its own name, / And toward fulfillment in the singleness of definition" (121).

For Warren the special appeal of the story was its connection with Thomas Jefferson, the fact that "the philosopher of our liberties and the architect of our country and the prophet of human perfectibility had this in the family blood."[8] And, for the writer absorbed with the problem of self-definition, the career of Jefferson possesses a special appropriateness. It is possible to argue, as Warren has, that it was Jefferson who defined, once and for all, the national character: "We suddenly had to define ourselves and what we stood for in one night. No other nation ever had to do that. In fact, one man did it—one man in an upstairs room, Thomas Jefferson."[9]

For nine years Warren was haunted by the story as he searched for a form adequate to his theme. The form of *Brother to Dragons* is unique, a kind of verse novel, the end-product of a series of mutations. Warren had first thought of a novel, but had decided that the story lacked the inevitability of narrative line necessary for the closed form of a novel. He feared that the enigma at the heart of the story would require a burden of commentary too heavy for the almost anecdotal nature of the plot. Warren and a collaborator began to fashion out a play in which Jefferson would have a choric role, but this plan too had to be abandoned because the role of Jefferson tended to overwhelm the material. The problem of finding an appropriate form even makes its way into the poem itself. The author, speaking as the character "R. P.W.," explains that he once intended to make a ballad of the story

> but the form
> Was not adequate: the facile imitation
> Of a folk simplicity would never serve,
> For the beauty of such simplicity is only
> That the action is always and perfectly self-contained. . . . (43)

"Then, at last," Warren said in a note on the composition of the poem, "I struck on the notion of using the form of a dramatic dialogue—not a play but a dialogue of all the characters, including Jefferson, at some unspecified place and time."[10] The idea of a dramatic dialogue with the setting—as the author's prefatory note informs us—"no place," and the time, "no time," opened up several possibilities. It allowed the author to "get out of the box of mere chronology" and to assess the meaning of the events not in a time-order of history but under the aspect of eternity. By considering the events out of time, Warren could also broaden the perspective to include commentary defining the meaning of the events for the modern world.

Jefferson is, as Warren has said, "the real protagonist."[11] Of course, the introduction of a character of Jefferson's stature would almost certainly dominate any work in which he appeared. To dare to put words into the mouth of the "spiritual father" of America would invite the criticism that a Founding Father would never talk in such a fashion—and such a criticism was promptly made. But if Warren did not write in a spirit of debunking, neither did he write out of a desire to whitewash the American past. Cutting short a satiric aside on the Daughters of the American Revolution, he dismisses the superpatriots in the only couplet in the poem: "But let that pass, for to the pious mind / Our history's nothing if it's not refined" (21). Jefferson speaks less than one-eighth of the lines in the poem and is seldom mentioned by the characters directly involved in the tragedy, yet his shadow falls ominously across the action, darkening and deepening its significance.

The Jefferson of Warren's poem had lived by a majestic dream of the perfectibility of man. He had been heartened by his belief in man's "natural innocence" which, released from its bondage to nature, would "dance like sunlight over the delighted landscape" (41). As a delegate to the Continental Congress, he had transcended self in the ecstasy of composing the Declaration of Independence and, effaced by a self-consuming flame, had seen man "angelic, arrogant, abstract" (9). For Jefferson, "blind with light" from the dazzling brilliance of his theory of human grandeur, the Maison Carrée at Nîmes is the symbol of the rational, balanced, and chaste beauty of the human mind, while the medieval cathedral, adorned with contorted and grotesque images of the human spirit, is a mere aberration of the "Gothic dark." But Lilburn's deed forces him to abandon his "outrageous dreams" and to conclude that "There's no forgiveness for our being human. / It's the inexpugnable error" (24).

Warren shows us the element of pride ("that flame in the personal darkness") in Jefferson's nature which is his tragic flaw. He speaks of "my West" and likens himself to a latter-day Moses destined to see that promised land only from afar. Because he is unprepared for the knowledge of man's, and particularly of his kinsman's, capacity for evil, his reaction to Lilburn's deed is shrill and furious, his earlier excessive optimism now inverted into a bleak pessimism. The awareness of man's essential evil turns human warmth into a delusion, love into a mask of mockery hiding the "immitigable ferocity of self," and life into the "unsummerable arctic of the human alienation" (47). In his extremity of rage and grief, Jefferson asserts that he would have murdered Lilburn with the same ease that Lilburn murdered the Negro slave, George. "The death of that black boy," Jefferson confesses, "was the death / Of all my hope" (132). Now, out of time and able to contemplate the sweep of American history, Jefferson can find abundant evidence to sustain his new pessimism: the appalling slaughter of the Civil War, the labor warfare at Haymarket Square and Detroit, the perversion of justice in the Sacco-Vanzetti case.

Although Jefferson dominates *Brother to Dragons* by virtue of his massive historical reputation, almost half the lines and most of the interpretative commentary are spoken by the author. The poet, R.P.W. ("red-headed, freckled, lean, a little stooped"), is, of course, a persona, yet there is evidently a large admixture of autobiography in the characterization. R.P.W. shares with an entire gallery of Warren characters the need "to be reconciled to the father's own reconciliation" (28). In a varied career he has been a "strayer and stranger" in many nations, and he has "shared the most common / Human experience which makes all mankind one"—isolation. R.P.W. finds mirrored in the story a reflection of his own struggle for meaning and fulfillment even though it is Jefferson who, like the Ancient Mariner in

Warren's interpretation, re-enacts the drama of repentance and rebirth. Within the poem the character of R.P.W. functions, in Warren's words, as a "kind of interlocutor," a center around which the action revolves and a focal point for its meaning. Like Jack Burden in *All the King's Men* and the narrator-historian in *World Enough and Time*, R.P.W. carefully culls the documents, sifts the facts from the folksay, and meditates on the ultimate meaning of the events. His manner is generally unassuming and deferential. His voice is subtly modulated, at times colloquial and racy, at others rising to a sweeping and impassioned rhetoric rich with echoes of Shakespeare and Milton. R.P.W. is, in short, part prompter, part commentator, and part participant in the action.

The controlling image of the poem is stated by Jefferson in one of his early speeches:

> The beast waits. He is the infamy of Crete.
> He is the midnight's enormity. He is
> Our brother, our darling brother. And Pasiphaë,
> Pasiphaë, huddled and hutched in the cow's hide,
> Laced, latched, thonged up, and humped for joy,
> What was the silence then before the stroke?
> And then your scream.   (7–8)

In the Greek myth, Pasiphaë became enamored of a bull and indulged her unnatural passion in a wooden cow built for her by Daedalus. The offspring of this union, the Minotaur, was half man and half bull. This terrible creature, housed in the Labyrinth, was eventually slain by Theseus.

The Minotaur-Labyrinth image expresses precisely the relationship of man to nature and of man to himself which is central to the theme of the poem. Each man is a labyrinth of his own devising, lost "in some blind lobby, hall, enclave, / Crank cul-de-sac, couloir, or corridor of time. / Of Time. Or self." (7) And within each man there lurks a minotaur, symbol of the bestial and monstrous connection of man with brute nature which he, like Theseus, must slay. As Pasiphaë satisfies her passion in a wooden cow, so man himself is trapped by his passion in an "infatuate machine" of his own invention.

Jefferson, bemused by his conception of natural innocence, had denied man's roots in nature. He had believed that "Man must redeem Nature" (37). R.P.W., however, accepts the familiar dualism of man's

nature, Pascal's ape and angel, Swift's Yahoo and Houyhnhnm. At the
mythological level, evil is the bestial in man; at the anagogical level, it
is his sin, his Original Sin. Man is, as the author of the Book of Job
asserts, a brother to dragons. For R.P.W. man's link with nature is his
opportunity for identity. To sink into nature is to sacrifice identity; to
be separate from nature is to achieve identity. Man must redeem not
nature but himself; and, paradoxically, the cost of his redemption is
isolation. "How can there be / Sensation," R.P.W. asks, "where there
is perfect adjustment?"

> The blood
> Of the creature is but the temperature of the sustaining flow:
> The catfish is in the Mississippi and
> The Mississippi is in the catfish and
> Under the ice both are at one with God.
> Would that we were!   (94)

Like the catfish, Lilburn has merged his identity with nature. At the
moment of the savage act, he abjures his humanity and appears, like
the earthquake which shakes the Mississippi Valley the same night, an
unleashed force of nature, "mindless, irreconcilable, absolute" (95).

We never hear Lilburn's own account of his actions. The two central
figures in the drama, Lilburn and George, each speak only once in the
poem. Lilburn utters a plaintive cry, a lament for the loss of light in
the encompassing darkness; George gives voice to his agony and bewilderment in the face of the event: "I was lost in my anguish, and I did
not know the reason" (194). Victor and victim, then, are left purposely
in shadow (indeed the question arises, who *is* victor and who victim);
and the meaning of the murderous act becomes the multiple truths of
the participants who join in the reconstruction of the event.

As each character relives his part in the drama, it becomes apparent
that the bloody act of hate has somehow stemmed from insufficient or
excessive love. Lilburn, who stands at the center of the story, is beloved
by all his immediate family, yet their love has not brought him salvation. His mother loved him, but in some obscure way she knows she
has failed him. "The human curse," she concludes, "is simply to love
and sometimes to love well, / But never well enough" (23). Lilburn's
love for her is a "black need," an obsession which is at the root of his
tangled dreams and perverse desires. His wife, Laetitia, loves him, but
he brutally defiles her by some unnamed and bestial perversion which

shocks and disgusts her. Laetitia, however, has also proved inadequate
to the demands of love. Like Pasiphaë "huddled and hutched in the
cow's hide," she had hungered for Lilburn. In partially willing the act,
she must, therefore, share the responsibility for her own violation. Lilburn's brother, Isham, "just loved Big Bubber" with mute adoration,
but Lilburn returns his love with carefully measured abuse and humil-
iation, saving Isham for the final betrayal at the grave's edge. Aunt
Cat, Lilburn's Negro Mammy, loves him with a grim possessiveness
and supernal cunning. Lilburn's rejection of her love leads her to
betray him to the sheriff ("Even love's a weapon," R.P.W. comments).

It is R.P.W. who points out that, paradoxically, Lilburn had done all
for love:

> For Love was all he asked, yet love
> Is the intolerable accusation of guilt
> To all the yearning Lilburns who cannot love,
> So must destroy who loves, and achieve at last
> The desiderated and ice-locked anguish of isolation.   (113)

R.P.W.'s interpretation of the act is strikingly similar to the narrator-
historian's analysis of Jeremiah Beaumont's motivation in *World
Enough and Time*. Lilburn yearns toward "the peace of definition"
and seeks that fulfillment in the "thrilling absoluteness of the pure act."
His own motives are unsullied, for the murder of George was

> done for good,
> For his mother and the sweetness of the heart,
> And that's the instructive fact of history,
> That evil's done for good, and in good's name—   (143)

Brother to Dragons moves toward its climax in the confrontation
scene of Jefferson and his sister, Lucy. Jefferson, absolving himself of
responsibility in the murder of George and condemning the immoral-
ity of his nephew's act, has concluded that the only reality is pain:

> We are born to joy that joy may become pain.
> We are born to hope that hope may become pain.
> We are born to love that love may become pain.
> We are born to pain that pain may become more
> Pain, and from that inexhaustible superflux
> We may give others pain as our prime definition—   (131–32)

For Lucy, however, love not pain is the index of self-definition and the measure of man's humanity. Without condoning the act, she is ready to accept her share of the responsibility. Jefferson is deaf to Lucy's plea that he extend his hand to Lilburn in a gesture of the mutual responsibility and guilt that binds all humanity. At this moment in the action, Meriwether Lewis, Jefferson's "near-son" and spiritual heir, suddenly appears to charge Jefferson with betrayal. Inspired by Jefferson's noble view of man's innocence, Meriwether had gone out "to redeem the wild world far to the Western Shore" (37). Dazzled by the vision of man's goodness, Meriwether had been ill-equipped for the evil he encountered on the trail, and his disillusionment had driven him to suicide.

Shaken by the charge, Jefferson acknowledges his complicity in Meriwether's suicide. Lucy then leads her brother to the knowledge that his kinship with Lilburn is deeper than blood. Jefferson's vision of man's "natural innocence" and Lilburn's "whirling dream of desperate innocence" are both equally remote from a world in which good and evil are irremediably fused. Just as Lilburn had seen in George his "darkest self / And all the possibility of the dark that he feared," so Jefferson's repudiation of Lilburn had sprung from an unconscious dread that he too might be "capable of all." Accepting this knowledge of self, Jefferson can now accept the knowledge which Jack Burden had so painfully won from his excursion into the past: "The dream of the future is not / Better than the fact of the past, no matter how terrible. / For without the fact of the past we cannot dream the future" (193).

It only remains for R.P.W. to ask the final question: "what is any knowledge / Without the intrinsic mediation of the heart?" (212). Standing on the bluff near the ruins of Rocky Hill, he watches the river roll onward like an image of the sweep of history, but an image only. For nature is "but mirror to the human heart's steadfast and central illumination" (211), and it is man who superimposes meaning onto nature. Five years earlier, in 1946, R.P.W. had come to that bluff. There in the ruined garden he had confronted evil, symbolized by a great black snake, *elaphe obsoleta obsoleta*. In the course of his excursion into the past, he had observed, ironically, that the modern world is "advanced / Beyond the superstitious fear of God's wrath" (64). Evil, however, is not so obsolete as the snake's name might imply. Each man holds within himself the "rich detritus of all History" (122), the burden of past evil and the possibility of future good. Now, in 1951, having come to terms with the story of Lilburn Lewis, R.P.W. is ready to reaffirm what he affirmed on his first trip to the bluff—the necessity of virtue:

> The recognition of complicity is the beginning of innocence.
> The recognition of necessity is the beginning of freedom.
> The recognition of the direction of fulfillment is the death of the self.
> And the death of the self is the beginning of selfhood.
> All else is surrogate of hope and destitution of spirit. (214–15)

Then R. P. W. descends the mountain and, like Jack Burden at the close of *All the King's Men*, is ready to enter "the world of action and liability."

Upon its appearance in 1953, several reviewers called *Brother to Dragons* Warren's finest achievement and the best long narrative poem produced by an American in this century. The intervening years since its publication have allowed the critical smoke to clear, but the passage of time has only served to confirm the early praise. In the novelty of its form, the freshness and flexibility of its idiom, and the narrative power of its blank verse, the poem seems to gain in stature and weight as the full measure of Warren's achievement becomes apparent. The poem clearly owes a debt to the earlier "Ballad of Billie Potts" in which Warren had alternated narrative and commentary, but in *Brother to Dragons* he has fused action and meaning in a way that carries the reader along on a rising wave of intellectual excitement.

Warren's great skill at characterization has never been more in evidence than in the pages of *Brother to Dragons*. Since his choice of a quasi-dramatic form meant the sacrifice of the usual expository and narrative devices for description and evocation of mood, the dialogue has to carry the entire burden of revealing character and forwarding action. Warren has managed to convey the unique flavor and slant of each character's speech while maintaining the unity of tone of the poem as a whole. The two women are particularly impressive. Lucy Lewis speaks with a firmly controlled eloquence which reflects her dignity and intelligence. Laetitia Lewis is less articulate, less profound; but her girlish and imploring appeals, couched in the vernacular of the frontier, are among the most touching passages in the poem. The same folk quality is carried over into the speech of Isham and Laetitia's brother: the one, matter-of-fact and rooted in concrete experience; the other, bumptious and arrogant. Counterpointing the speech of these

characters is the haunting and earthy dialect of Aunt Cat. The speech
of all the characters is unified by the pervasive imagery of light and
dark, sun and shade (anticipated in the epigraph from Lucretius)
which suggests, at one level, the polarities of knowledge and ignorance
and, at another level, glory and damnation. Our lives must be worked
out neither in the sunlit dazzle of innocence nor in the opaque darkness
of malignant nature but "in the shade of the human condition" (193).[12]

III   Band of Angels

Brother of Dragons was greeted with enthusiasm and respect by the
critics. But when it was followed in 1955 by *Band of Angels*, a novel
also set in nineteenth-century Kentucky, the cry went up that Warren
had relaxed his standards. The fact that a motion picture was soon
made from the novel seemed to substantiate the criticism. Warren's
very considerable narrative powers were at full stretch, and *Band of
Angels*, the critics charged, was melodrama beyond the dreams of
Margaret Mitchell.

"History," Warren has said, "is not melodrama, even if it usually
reads like that."[13] If *Band of Angels* reads like melodrama, it is because
of the novel's faithfulness to history. Warren told Leonard Casper that
he drew upon Winston Coleman's *Slavery Days in Kentucky* and
Theodore Canot's *Adventures of an African Slaver*, as well as upon
memoirs of officers on slave patrol, hearings in the British Parliament,
and other documents from the Brown University and Yale University
collections.[14]

Warren has, however, evoked the past not for its own sake but for
the way in which it at once reflects and illuminates his characters. And
Warren can evoke the past. He understands, as he demonstrated in
World Enough and Time, the ways of the historical imagination and
energizes them with the novelist's art. *Band of Angels* draws on the
epochal events of American history in a way that *World Enough and
Time* did not. John Brown strikes at Harpers Ferry, men die at Shiloh,
the noose draws tighter about New Orleans, Farragut runs the forts.
The guns, however, boom faintly on the periphery of the novel, threatening but distant. The decisive public events are transmuted by Warren into symbols of personal histories. The conflicts that rage on the
battlefield, the emancipation of the slaves, the horrors of Reconstruction—all have their counterparts in the soul of the novel's heroine,
Amantha Starr. As she says early in the novel:

You live through time, that little piece of time that is yours, but that piece of time is not only your own life, it is the summing-up of all the other lives that are simultaneous with yours. It is, in other words, History, and what you are is an expression of History, and you do not live your life, but somehow your life lives you, and you are, therefore, only what History does to you. (112)

True, but only a partial truth, because as Amantha comes to see, "You are, also, what you do to History."

Warren's initial impulse for the novel was a story, well known in Kentucky, of a wealthy Lexington widower who fathered two daughters by his quadroon concubine. The girls, bred to freedom, are seized at his grave by his creditors and sold down-river, at which point they disappear from history. What drew Warren to the episode was their father's inability to face the fact that his daughters were not white. He was incapable of denominating them slaves, a necessary step to manumission. *Band of Angels*, Warren said, "is about an investigation of the nature of freedom. I mean she's never free-you can't set her free from the fact of the relationship to the father. Until she can forgive her father, she's not free."[15]

Out of dramatic necessity Warren coalesced the two girls into one, and it is from the point of view of Amantha Starr, the daughter of a Kentucky planter and his Negro slave, that the reader sees the story. The opening sentences of the first two paragraphs state the central theme: first, Amantha's imploring questions, "Oh, who am I?" followed by her cry, "if I could only be free." These are but a new set of terms for a working out of the by now familiar Warren problem, the problem of identity. Amantha is seeking to define herself or, as she puts it, "to make myself come true."

Amantha Starr is a singularly passive character, defined in large measure by the men who surround her. She tells her story with candor and modesty, but like those other—very different because more knowing—heroines of fiction Elizabeth Bennett and Becky Sharp, part of her charm is that she is desired by almost every man she meets. Amantha freely confesses acts of cowardice and disloyalty, disarmingly reveals that she knows the "sweet advantage of having been little and precious and wronged," yet her innocence and the pathos of her plight relieve her actions of any tinge of malice. As she enters into each new liaison, she gropes toward identity only to suffer again the "terror of abandonment."

Band of Angels opens with an evocation of childhood, the first nine years of Amantha's life on a Kentucky plantation. These events are remembered "only in portentous disconnection, each in a kind of mystic isolation." This static, selective quality of memory carries over into adulthood. Amantha persists in remembering her life in snapshot glimpses frozen in memory until the shock of events causes her to see the past as a dynamic, shaping force in the present, for she wants her private history "to be fixed in the darkness of the past." She must learn that the darkness of the past is a "teeming darkness, straining soundlessly with forms struggling for recognition, for release from that dark realm of undifferentiated possibility" (218).

The crucial event remembered from Amantha's childhood is an episode with an old family retainer named Shadrach. While jouncing the child on his lap, Shadrach is told by her Mammy that Amantha is too old for such fondling. Trapped and enraged by the innuendo and aware that Amantha is the child of a mother who was neither white nor free, Shadrach pushes her contemptuously away, saying, "Yeah— what she?" When Amantha innocently relates the incident to her father, he summarily sells the old Negro, but not before Shadrach attempts to escape and is brutally beaten by his captors. Bewildered by the event, Amantha has the first hint of the "giddy insubstantiality" of childhood innocence. She is guiltily aware that she has somehow betrayed Shadrach's love and spat upon the "niggerness" in him. But as a legacy, Shadrach has left her with a question, "What she?" (13).

Amantha is taken to Cincinnati by her father where, under the tutelage of the sensuous and worldly Miss Idell, she is outfitted for Oberlin College. Miss Idell, foil to Amantha, plays gaily and successfully the roles of Mrs. Muller, Mrs. Starr, and Mrs. Morton. But she remains always in her own mind, as in the fancy of Amantha, Miss Idell. She is another of those secure and masterful Warren characters whose "certainty of self" is the despair and envy of the seekers for self-knowledge. In contrast to Miss Idell's confidence is Amantha's diffidence, embodied in the recurring images of dreaming and of the receding immensity of sky.

At Oberlin Amantha meets and falls in love with an ascetic theology student, Seth Parton; and from him she learns to mouth the pious clichés of Abolition—the argument from righteousness, the argument of self-interest. At Oberlin she also absorbs the pastoral vision of blacks in their native Africa: "the sweet village where the flowers brilliantly bloomed and beloved faces lifted to greet them from the shadow of tiny beehive shaped grass huts" (62). Amantha, typically assuming the protective coloration of the environment into which she is thrust, is converted to Abolition and promptly challenges her father to free his slaves, oblivious to the irony that she is requiring of him her own freedom. Seeing his bumbling embarrassment in framing a reply, she feels "some hard sense of advantage just gained" (27). This tentative assertion of her identity—her newfound power over her father and the flattering attentions of Seth—vanishes with the crushing news that her father has died, an adulterer and, so rumor has it, an embezzler.

Returning to Kentucky to her father's funeral, Amantha is arrested by the sheriff at the grave to satisfy the claims made against her father's estate. Her father, torn between his guilt-ridden need to set free "little Manty" and his unwillingness to declare her less than his own child, had never drawn up the manumission papers. As a result, the terms of her self-definition are enlarged by two other men: the sheriff who gives her a legal definition, "female property,"· and the slave trader who gives her an economic one, "a nigger is what you can sell." She is thus reduced to chattel, a "non-person . . . suspended in the vacuum of no identity" (52). She proclaims her hatred of her father as, in the course of the novel, she proclaims, coldly and almost ritualistically, her hatred of each of the men in her life. Sold down the river like Shadrach, screaming and struggling, she sinks into a luxury she will continue to allow herself, the luxury of self-pity.

At New Orleans, Amantha is bought at auction by an aging cotton planter, Hamish Bond, whose name suggests both the biblical progenitor of the black race, Ham, and the ties that hold Amantha. Bond impulsively buys her, impelled in part by his urge to possess her and in part by a sense of pity. (He has, his former mulatto mistress remarks, "kindness like a disease.") Bond shares his creator's gift for language, and the account of his life—the familiar Warren pattern of a plot within a plot and a virtuoso display of his storytelling powers—is a harrowing version of the barbarism out of which the slaves came, a corrective to the idyllic picture of Africa that Amantha had learned at Oberlin.

Amantha's role in Bond's household is highly equivocal. He indulges her whims and makes no sexual demands upon her at first, but this illusory freedom only serves to accentuate the peculiar hold he has on her and the ambiguity of her racial composition. Legally a black, she can yet dream of an escape northward to "be lost in a world of white faces" (91). Amantha longs to have Bond decisively define her life, but he, like her father, cannot bring himself to free her for fear he will cease to possess her.

Amantha's life with Bond follows a pattern remarkably similar to her life at her father's plantation. In each instance, there is a terrifying storm which leads to a personal revelation, a plantation jubilee, and a romantic involvement. Each relationship is defined by an incident in which an older man leaps quixotically to the protection of a young girl, from which she gains "some hard secret sense of advantage" (135). In their cyclical pattern, these events emphasize Amantha's insistence on preserving inviolate her image of "Little Manty." Her own self-pity encourages her father and Bond to luxuriate in feelings of condescension toward her. The death of her father meant the end of the secure world of her childhood. As the Confederacy topples, her life with Hamish Bond collapses. Bond sets Amantha "free" in war-torn New Orleans only to return after the city is under martial law to ask her to marry him. By this time, however, she is engaged to marry one of the "liberators," a Union officer named Tobias Sears.

The tension in Amantha's mind concerning her race is manifested not only by her relationship with the men around her but also by Warren's varied and complex handling of black-white imagery. The reader is constantly aware that the action is unfolding against the dazzling white of the cotton fields with the ominous blackness of the forests as a backdrop. At her father's funeral, Amantha is struck by "the ladies in black, . . . the faces white and staring at me," a memory that returns to haunt her. There is the Dantesque scene of a black being prepared for the slave market in a tub of scalding water, "the vapor wreathing up whitely about his black skinniness." And in her despair Amantha cries, when offered a lamp by a servant, "For me, it's all the same! Light or dark" (78).

This black-white polarity is maintained in the contrast of Hamish Bond's two associates who desire Amantha, Rau-Ru and Charles Prieur-Denis. Rau-Ru is the *K'la*, a favored overseer at Bond's upriver plantation and a kind of secret sharer or alter ego. When Amantha first sees him she is struck by the "face of preternatural blackness, like enameled steel, against the white of the loose blouse." Although Rau-Ru achieves his own freedom, Amantha associates him with the world of slavery from which she would gladly escape. Set off against Rau-Ru is Charles Prieur-Denis, "a figure in white trousers and black coat of silky sheen." His elegant and exotic manner disguises a sharper, swindler, and slave-runner who would use Bond's plantation for a barracoon. Bond, "to test his weakness," perversely throws his "pore little Manty" and Charles together, but Charles's attempt at a seduction is thwarted by Rau-Ru. Charles is gravely injured in the resulting fracas, and Rau-Ru, denied a hearing in court because of his color, flees to the forest. As these men destroy themselves for her, Amantha remains aloof, singularly passive and uncomprehending: "I was thinking of my own suffering, my disarray of spirit, my disorientation and fear."

The concluding section of the novel takes as its theme Amantha's effort to find identity through her marriage to Tobias Sears. Sears, an Emersonian of the Brahmin stamp, is yet another of the familiar Warren clan of uncompromising idealists which includes Percy Munn, Adam Stanton, and Jeremiah Beaumont. He speaks mistily of his devotion to the "idea" beyond the realities of this world. He has, Amantha says, "nobility like a disease."

Determined to devote his life to the cause of freeing the slaves, he insists on a black command during the Civil War, and after Appomattox accepts a post in the Freedman's Bureau. Like Jack Burden, Tobias loves Truth, but his truth has a way of being the obverse of the truth of those he suspects of having influence over him. With Tobias, Amantha hopes to "start life over, to make our world of loving kindness." Her decision is a renewed affirmation of identity founded on the denial of her personal history. She will cancel the past with a resolution.

But Tobias fails—"failing westward," in Amantha's phrase— infected by the materialism of Reconstruction which attracts him even while it repels him. Nor is he able to reconcile the idealism of his great crusade for Negro rights with the reality of a wife whose mother was a slave. Such self-knowledge as he is granted comes while he is engaged in the seriocomic reclamation of the black garbage collector of Halesburg, Kansas. It is only when Tobias sees himself reflected in the pitying and contemptuous glance of a rich black from Chicago—sees himself, that is, not as "the bearer of freedom" of his imagination but as the drunkard and failure that he is—can he affirm the brotherhood of the dispossessed. In a moment of illumination, he discovers he has deluded himself and demeaned his wife. With Tobias's abdication of his role as "liberator," Amantha can now proclaim her own emancipation, for she has discovered that dependence is a trap and "nobody can set you free . . . except yourself" (303). "Don't ever call me little Manty again," she tells Tobias and, at a stroke, discards the protective, self-pitying image which has been the prop of a lifetime and enters into the "awfulness of joy."

Readers have complained, with some justification, of this flat and anticlimactic ending. The "joy" which cancels the "old shadows" is unconvincing, for Amantha's ultimate illumination seems in excess of the struggles which precipitated it. Amantha herself is not so persuasive as other Warren *raisonneurs*. We are asked to believe in the essential passivity of her character even when it seems strongly at variance with the speculative bent of her mind. It strains credibility to believe that a character so reflective can at the same time be so insensitive. Her experience, moreover, is not developed with sufficient depth and vividness to make convincing the psychological states through which she passes.

Finally, the attention lavished on the novel's interior decoration detracts from the total effect. Warren has always had "a romantic kind of interest in the objects of American history—saddles, shoes, figures of speech."[16] He knows the heft of a Civil War rifle, the cut of a Yankee officer's coat, the look of a Baltimore clipper as it slips down the Patapsco River. In *Band of Angels*, however, there is such a clutter of detail, such an insistence on background authenticity, that the reader may feel—as does the visitor to some widely heralded historical restoration—that the scene has everything but the breath of life. Even antiquarian zeal cannot compensate for the flaws which make *Band of Angels* the least satisfactory of Warren's excursions into American history.

IV   Wilderness

Since *Band of Angels* Warren has written only one historical novel. In 1961 as the country entered upon a four-year binge of nostalgia commemorating the Civil War Centennial, he published *Wilderness: A Tale of the Civil War*. Its appearance brought to a conclusion more than a decade in which he had, as he likes to say, "soaked" himself in American history.

Episodic in structure, *Wilderness* departs radically in form from the earlier novels, varying in the direction of greater simplicity. Gone are the brooding disquisitions on truth and history, for Warren has, as his critics have so long advised, dropped his passages of philosophizing in favor of a direct and uncluttered narrative. Nor is the novel, as the seasoned reader of Warren might expect, set wholly in the South. *Wilderness* opens in Bavaria, then shifts to New York City. Its protagonist, a Jewish clock repairer, seems at first an unusual addition to Warren's lengthening dramatis personae. But as he has said, "Jewish writing in America has a minority psychology, so does Southern writing. . . . There's a certain *insideness* of the *outsider*, and intensities of inside effects sometimes look queer to those who are not inside."[17]

Thematically, however, the novel returns to a favorite Warren problem—the idealist, bemused by the "compulsion of the dream," who is forced to test his vision of reality against the "gigantic conspiracy" of the world. Since a great war would, by its nature, both magnify and simplify the issues involved, Warren has dramatized the dilemma of the idealist by thrusting him into the American Civil War. Finding in the tensions and contradictions of the war an outer manifestation of the inner lives of his characters, Warren wrote in his long essay *The Legacy of the Civil War*: "In a civil war . . . all the self-divisions of conflicts within individuals become a series of mirrors in which the plight of the country is reflected, and the self-division of the country a great mirror in which the individual may see imaged his own deep conflicts, not only the conflicts of political loyalties, but those more profoundly personal."[18]

Having treated the idealist heretofore in a mocking or ironic fashion, Warren draws Adam Rosensweig, the hero of *Wilderness*, with obvious warmth and sympathy. Adam, a cripple doomed from birth with a deformed foot, seems destined to live out his life repairing watches in a stagnant Bavarian town where, ironically, time stands still. But determining to go to America to "fight for freedom," he has Old Jacob, the village cobbler, fashion him a special boot braced with straps and buckles which makes him "look almost like anybody else" (17). Jacob, who through adversity has entered into the "awfulness of joy" (31), refuses to take payment for the boot—it is his own investment in the cause of freedom. "You may wear it into battle," he tells Adam, "but it will still be mine" (32). When Adam reveals his plan to his uncle he is dismissed as a fool—a judgment of Adam repeated by every major character in the novel. But there is nothing to hold Adam in Bavaria: his parents are dead, his father's only legacy a love of liberty and an incapacity for serving his own worldly interests. With a satchel containing phylactery, talith, and siddur, the gift of his devout uncle, Adam signs on for America with a boatload of mercenaries.

Adam's idealism is put to the test at once when the recruiter, Duncan, discovers the deformity. Adam insists that his foot would not

hinder him in combat, but Duncan, enraged before such naked idealism, refuses to allow him to debark at New York. At this juncture
Adam speculates on the uselessness of his two gifts from Bavaria—the
satchel with the objects of devotion and the boot. They came to him in
"balanced and mutual inimicalness," for he cannot pray and he will
never march for freedom. An anonymous sailor, however, who wishes
only to see "if a thing could be done," contrives Adam's escape from
the ship. When Adam, thinking to find in his partisan a fellow idealist,
tactlessly presses him for his real motive, the sailor blurts out, "ye are
a ruddy fool." Ironically, Adam's crippled foot, while heightening his
awareness of his difference from other men, makes him curiously
insensitive to them.

Once Adam is free in New York, his idealism is further tested by
the discovery that not all Yankees are selflessly dedicated to black freedom. Rather than wanting to die to make men free, they are demonstrating against conscription by lynching every black they can find.
Caught up in the riots raging in the city, Adam is saved from death at
the hands of the mob by a black, Mose Talbutt, who gets him safely to
the home of Aaron Blaustein. When Adam tells Blaustein, a friend of
his uncle in Bavaria, of his plan to join the army, the older man looks
pityingly at the deformed foot, seeing in it the congenital defect all
men have at birth. "There is always something from birth," he tells
Adam. "There is yourself" (71).

Unable to persuade Adam to stay with him in New York, Blaustein
finds Adam a place as assistant to a sutler, Jed Hawksworth, who is
leaving for the South. Hawksworth, a North Carolinian who had been
driven from the South years earlier for daring to defend a falsely
accused slave, despises in Adam the idealism he himself has long since
repudiated. The story of Jed's selfless act strikes a responsive chord in
Adam, but he finds he cannot admire or even respect his sullen
employer. Mose Talbutt, who, it develops, is a runaway slave and
deserter, accompanies them as Jed's other assistant. Mose rechristens
Adam "Slew" for his deformity, thus initiating Adam's search for identity in the usual fashion of Warren heroes. Adam pities Mose and tries
to help him, but he can feel no warmth for him as an individual.

Adam's experiences on the trip to the lines seem to challenge the
worth of his pilgrimage and of his father's teaching that there is no
nobler fate than to die for human liberty. At a farm where the three
men camp, Adam comes upon a German immigrant, a man much like
himself, who lies dying of a wound received at Chancellorsville. As he

sits by the man's bedside, sickened by the stench of the suppurating wound, Adam becomes aware of the apparent futility of the man's actions. At Gettysburg, only months after the battle, Adam listens to a drunken harangue on the better part of valor from the Falstaffian Mordacai Sulgrave. When the three men finally reach the army in winter quarters, Adam is further discountenanced by the aimless violence and casual lusts of the liberators. The Federal soldiers are as cynical, coarse, and prejudice-ridden as are, apparently, the men of the Confederacy. But Adam continues to search for some "way to affirm his history and identity in the torpid, befogged loneliness" of America (163).

The three men, each in his own way an outcast, become more deeply involved in their reciprocal needs. Jed increasingly relies on his two assistants, and in his dependence comes to despise the quiet competence of Adam and the sullen arrogance of Mose. Jed torments Mose until, goaded beyond endurance, Mose murders him. Earlier the same night Mose, on his part, had driven Adam to curse him savagely. Mose flees after the murder, and Adam, wondering guiltily why he was not the victim, concludes that "Mose had not been able to kill him because he had once saved him" (302).

When the murder of Jed and the consequent flight of Mose leave Adam suddenly "free" in the wilderness of Virginia, he begins to perceive dimly that his desire to fight for freedom is, like the quest of Amantha Starr, but the inversion of his need to set himself free. He starts down the trail alone with the sutler's wagon, but his newly found freedom brings him only a curious sense of devaluation, "of sad ghostliness." In the isolation that defines him, he feels his identity draining away. Stopping in a silent glade where the Battle of the Wilderness rages about him, Adam feels himself in the "cold center of stillness in the storm which was the world" (290).

While musing on the chain of circumstance that brought him from Bavaria to a scrub forest in a hostile land, he is surprised by several tattered and barefoot Confederate soldiers who plunge into the glade, strip him of his boots, and commandeer his supplies. Adam, watching these defenders of slavery ravenously devouring his food, feels a warm gush of pity and blesses them unawares. Abruptly, Union soldiers charge into the glade, and in the melee, Adam seizes a rifle and kills one of the Confederate "scarecrows," a man of "most commonplace face." The eruption of violence, the frenzied and senseless slaughter, subsides as quickly as it began, and Adam is left in the glade with his victim at his feet.

Adam again reflects on the forces which have led him to this point in his odyssey. Instead of dying for liberty, he is himself stained with the blood of a Confederate soldier. He is suddenly filled with the desolating knowledge that he has been a victim, betrayed by everything and everyone in whom he had believed. And in a sudden excess of anguish he glimpses the black depths of his own motivation: "*I killed him*, he thought, *because his foot was not like mine*." Hardened by this new knowledge, Adam coldly reaches down to pull the boots off the feet of the dead soldier. They are, he sees, Union boots, so the Confederate must have taken them from a Federal soldier. "*Now it is my turn*," Adam thinks. Starting to put on the boots, he catches sight of the satchel with its phylactery and talith. Somehow they survived the vicissitudes of his life in America and now lie strewn across the ground. At the sight, Adam's new found sense of power and mastery dies within him. As if to define the terms of his dilemma, Adam stands between boot and satchel, his legacy from Bavaria. He looks again into the face of the dead man. "Am I different from other men?" he asks himself. And then he finds himself suddenly able to pray: "Have mercy upon the remnant of the flock of Thy hand, and say unto the Destroying Angel, Stay thy hand" (309).

Adam knows that now he will put on the boots, not Old Jacob's boots that make him "look almost like anybody else," but ordinary boots worn by anonymous men of both armies: "He could try, he thought, to be worthy of their namelessness, out of what they, as men and in their error, had endured." He will put on the boots not in vindictiveness and arrogance, but in humility and recognition of the human communion. He is at last reconciled to his own past; he would live it all over again but, as he cries out, "*with a different heart!*"

Wilderness is developed with an economy of means rare in Warren's fiction. The long case histories, the garrulous reminiscences, the diaries and journals of his early novels are missing. He has always had a tendency to let minor characters seize control of the narrative and, with their own fascinating histories, elbow the star from the center of the stage. But in *Wilderness* the minor characters are rigorously subordinated to the central concerns of the hero.

In retrospect, however, Warren became dissatisfied with his hero, believing that his personal growth did not keep pace with the development of the experiences he was undergoing. "You have the strange effect," he told Marshall Walker, "of a central *hollowness* with a rich context, with the central character as an observer who is a mere observer. He's involved intellectually, but only intellectually. The story is never fleshed out in enough depth so that the world of context is related to his experience in the right way."[19]

In Adam Rosensweig, the Old World Innocent adrift in a corrupt New World, Warren has reversed the roles made familiar by so many heroes of Henry James; for, paradoxically, some "fantastic innocence" (206) is necessary for a European to plumb the depths of American corruption. And Warren evidently intends Adam to be representative of a type, described in *The Legacy of the Civil War*, which he believes to be increasingly rare in modern America: "Those men from conflict and division rose to strength. From complication they made the simple cutting edge of action. They were, in the deepest sense, individuals; that is, by moral awareness they had achieved, in varying degrees, identity."[20]

CHAPTER 6

A Life Record

ROBERT PENN WARREN returned to the writing of poetry after a dry spell that lasted a decade. In 1969 he told an interviewer: "I didn't finish a single short poem for ten years, from '45—God, it must have been '44 or '45, along in there—until '54 . . . I must have started fifty short poems. Not one panned out. I couldn't finish them; they died on me." Forced to reassess his approach to the writing of verse, Warren revised fundamentally his notion of what for him constituted the germ of a poem. "When I went back to writing short poems," he said, "the poems were more directly tied to a realistic base of facts. . . . They were closer to me, closer to my observed and felt life."[1]

I Promises, Poems 1954–1956

The first harvest of this reassessment was *Promises, Poems 1954–1956*. More warmly received than any book he had written since *All the King's Men*, *Promises* won the Pulitzer Prize, the National Book Award, and the Edna St. Vincent Millay Award of the Poetry Society of America. Like his earlier poetry, the poems in *Promises* are written in a variety of verse forms—sonnets, lullabies, lyrics, and, in "Dragon Country," a variation on the tall tale of the frontier. These poems manifest the same technical resources and speak with the same directness as Warren's earlier verse. His recognition of "our time's sad declension" is still evident, as is his acute sense of disillusionment, his insistence that human nature is fundamentally perverse and endlessly paradoxical. But *Promises*, as its title suggests, also speaks quietly of a "sunlit chance" and a "dawning perspective and possibility of human good." The lines are vibrant with a warmth at variance with the crabbed intellectuality of some of Warren's earlier poetry. Offering neither easy consolation nor glib evasion, these poems are a mature recognition of the terror of the human condition and the possibility of ultimate triumph over it. The recognition springs from an apprehension of the "necessity of truth," and the possibility of triumph from the knowledge that "there's natural distress / In learning to face Truth's glare-glory."

These insights are couched in a form which, in contrast to the scoured, burnished verses of the earlier poetry, has a greater ease of movement and a more varied rhythm. The cold perfection of some of Warren's earlier poetry is replaced by a studied roughening. Having demonstrated his mastery of traditional forms, Warren has tried to go beyond them at the risk of being charged with ineptitude and cacophony. In reaching out for new effects, he may have had in mind a quality he noted in Melville's poetry: "Perhaps the violences, the distortions, the wrenchings in the versification of some of the poems are to be interpreted as . . . a conscious effort to develop a nervous, dramatic, masculine style."[2]

Promises is distinctly personal in tone and subject matter, and in this respect the volume follows the direction already foreshadowed in *Brother to Dragons.* Even though Warren's preoccupation with certain plot situations and character types betokens a source in his own experience, he had always fully assimilated the materials and subordinated them to his intention. In *Promises,* however, Warren seems impelled to exploit the materials of his experience directly. The personal note is struck immediately in the dedications to the two sections of the volume: the first to Warren's daughter, Rosanna, "a little girl, one year old, in a ruined fortress," and the second to his son, Gabriel.

The sequence of five poems to Rosanna which opens the volume is set on a stretch of Italian seashore north of Rome where Warren and his wife have taken their daughter. The first three poems, written in a loose variation of the sonnet form, describe a sun-drenched landscape of vineyards sweeping down to a sand beach sheltered from the waves by black lava chunks. On a sea-cliff overlooking the Mediterranean, a fortress, once the symbol of a Spanish monarch's power, is now reduced to a rubble of stones overgrown with golden gorse and thistle. Near the fortress lives the *gobbo*—the hunchback—with his sullen, glaring wife. Seven of their children play in the dirt outside the house; the eighth is defective, the result of the mother's unsuccessful attempt at abortion. About the scene is the aura of an old and spent civilization, the sense of time and history stretching endlessly backward. The "classic pose" of an engaged couple, the "triptych beauty" of the *gobbo*'s little girl who is "beautiful like a saint," and the predominant tones of gold and blue remind us of a magnificent Italian past in contrast to the ugliness of the present—garbage in the moat, the "monster" child next door. Against this background of an incredibly ancient and "ruined world" is the laughing and golden-haired Rosanna, innocent and vulnerable, a symbol of promise and renewal.

"The Flower," the fourth poem of the series, is a little parable that embodies the controlling idea of the volume—the promise, a covenant between the generations that will be abrogated or fulfilled. Each day at twilight as the poet, his wife, and their daughter climb from the beach to the hill fortress, they come to a favorite spot in the path where the child always demands a white flower to carry in her hand. The parents share her childlike delight in the ritual, and in token of their own happiness, the mother every afternoon since early June has put a blue flower in the child's yellow hair. As the season wanes, the flowers fade, and inevitably the day arrives when there is no bloom "worthily white." But the little girl still insists on even a "ruined" flower and sings "as though human need / Were not for perfection." The poet, musing on the child's joyous acceptance, can suspend for a moment his adult fears of a multiform world of flux and change and, in the simple innocence of the scene before him, can proclaim the oneness of human life:

> And in that image let
> Both past and future forget,
> In clasped communal ease,
> Their brute identities.

As he ascends the hill, the poet looks back once more toward the bay and watches a white gull turn suddenly black against the sunset, then circle back toward the east. The poet follows the arc of the bird's flight and, in the moment before it dips below the mountain, sees it gleam suddenly and hopefully white in the last light. As darkness falls, the poet and child hear the familiar rustling of the surf with its promise of a new dawn.

Among the series of poems dedicated to his infant son, Gabriel, are several which have Italian settings linking them to the Rosanna sequence, but in general the poems to Gabriel are grounded in the South of Warren's youth. In "Hands Are Paid," for example, the speaker recalls a single working day in the life of a farmhand. The scene, Warren's boyhood Kentucky, returns to him in all its specificity:

sweat-cold overalls, a mule's head at the barn-lot bar, the clatter of a red thresher. The farmhand comes home exhausted, eats his sowbelly and cornbread, kicks off his shoes, and falls heavily into bed. Remembering the scene on a "foreign shore," the speaker names over each item "but cannot think / What in their urgency, they must mean." The Gabriel sequence constitutes an effort to determine that meaning.

The search for the meaning of the past is nothing new in Warren, but the renewed urgency of his quest springs from the need to define the world of his youth not only to his own satisfaction but also to that of his son. Ranging backward to encompass Warren's parents as well as the southern heritage in its broader reaches, these poems, in their personal aspects, constitute a legacy to Gabriel from all who have gone before. In the opening poem, "What Was the Promise That Smiled from the Maples at Evening?" the poet's father, Robert Franklin Warren, speaks from the grave to all succeeding generations: "We died only that every promise might be fulfilled." In "Founding Fathers, Nineteenth Century Style, Southeast U.S.A.," the names made familiar by the textbooks—Sam Houston, James Bowie, Henry Clay—speak across the years, as do others unknown to fame. Among them are two of Warren's own ancestors, a land shark "not well trusted" and a crusty old veteran of Shiloh. They offer no advice for our "complexity of choices, / But beg us only one word to justify their own old life-cost."

Among the most memorable poems in *Promises* are the verse narratives. These poems might have been cast as short stories twenty years earlier, but Warren declared in 1959 that he would write no more short fiction. "Poems," he said at that time, "are great devourers of short stories."[3] Both "School Lesson" and "Country Burying (1919)" are typical Warren short stories distilled into verse. At least two poems, "Court-martial" and "Dark Night of the Soul," are retellings of earlier stories, themselves among Warren's best.

"Dark Night of the Soul" is a return to the experience already realized in "Blackberry Winter." A twelve-year-old boy, bookish, curious, innocent, sees an old and grizzled tramp lurking in the forest bordering his father's farm. Going to fetch the cows, the boy comes suddenly upon the tramp who is lying exhausted in a clump of honeysuckle. Their eyes "thread the single thread / Of the human entrapment" until the tramp pitifully begs the boy to get away. But since the child, entranced by the pathos of the tramp's condition, cannot tear his eyes away, the old man stumbles to his feet and continues his journey which "no man would have planned." In contrast to "Blackberry Winter,"

"Dark Night of the Soul" grants the moment of illumination not to the boy but to the tramp. Having experienced the "absolute and glacial purity of despair," the tramp is able to enter into the "awfulness of joy," but exactly how or why we are not told.

"Court-martial" delineates the relationship of a boy and his grandfather that is not unlike the one Warren explored in his story "When the Light Gets Green." The poem is concerned with the boy's efforts to "untie / The knot of History." Under the eyes of the old captain of cavalry, the child with his toy soldiers fights again the campaigns of the Civil War, certain that "death is only the glory." A chance question elicits from the old man a brutal tale of court-martialing guerrillas. "Two lieutenants talk law," and then, without mercy or compunction, the guerrillas were taken to the woods and hanged. The rapt, horrified stare of the little boy at the disclosure wrings from the old man an involuntary cry of conscience. In the "darkening air" the child's unblemished image of his grandfather is shattered, and the boy realizes that he, in his innocence, has passed judgment on his grandfather's guilt.

II   You, Emperors, and Others

Promises was followed in 1960 by *You, Emperors, and Others, Poems 1957–1960*, which is linked to the earlier volume in both theme and form. The lyric "Debate: Question, Quarry, Dream" recalls the Gabriel sequence, speaking as it does of an infant son and his father's "appalling logic of joy." And the satiric, slangy idiom of "Nocturne" and "Man in the Street" relates them to "Ballad of a Sweet Dream of Peace" in *Promises*. Although *You, Emperors, and Others* lacks the thematic unity of *Promises*, the later volume offers a wider variety of formal effects. In addition to lullabies and verse narratives, there are parodies of nursery rhymes, epigrams, an elegy, and a ballad.

You, Emperors, and Others takes its title from the two groups of poems which open the volume. In the first, an eight-poem series entitled "Garland for You," the central concern is the search for definition: the need "To recognize / The human self naked in your own eyes." The *you* of the poems is everyman, the face staring back from the mirror that one cannot meet or, meeting, cannot recognize. The poem may address the man in the "Ivy League flannel suit," "Mr. and Mrs. North and South America," or, as in the second series entitled "Two Pieces after Suetonius," the emperors Domitian and Tiberius. It is apparent, however, that, as the opening poem declares, "Whoever you are, this poem is clearly about you."

The most ambitious series in *You, Emperors, and Others,* "Mortmain," is a cycle of five poems dealing with the poet's father. "Mortmain" represents still another variation on the theme of the poems to Gabriel in *Promises.* In that sequence the birth of his son has led the poet to examine his childhood. In "Mortmain" the death of his father forces upon him a reexamination of the past and its meaning. The memories of his father's youth with its early promise and inevitable disappointments are rendered more poignant by the poet's small son who, surrounded by a teddy bear and letter blocks, laughs from a farther room. "I / Do not want to weep," the poet says, "I want to understand."

The title of the opening poem of "Mortmain" speaks with the blunt insistence of a newspaper headline: "After Night Flight Son Reaches Bedside of Already Unconscious Father, Whose Right Hand Lifts in a Spasmodic Gesture, As Though Trying to Make Contact: 1955." The poem opens with a series of images all pointing to the idea of order. The poet has rushed by plane in "Time's concatenation" across the "abstract flight-grid of sky." Arriving at the bedside, he watches his father's waxy hand claw up "like law" from the "ritualistically reordered" covers. In contrast to these images of pattern and order are the hysterical disconnections of the poet's mind:

> . . . *oh, oop-si-daisy,* churns
> The sad heart, *oh, atta-boy, daddio's got*
> *One more shot in the locker, peas-porridge hot—*

Through such abrupt shifts in tone, Warren communicates the strain of attempting to hold in check a mind plunged into deep grief, a technique which recalls an earlier poem on the same theme, "The Return: An Elegy." In a single gesture of recognition and loss, the relationship of father and son is brought into focus. The feeble hand of the father holds within it the son's own life, and the son's affirmation of selfhood—the "I" which the meter of the poem continually thrusts at the reader—is negated by the father's gesture, leaving the son "Naked in that black blast of his love."

In the concluding poem of the "Mortmain" series, the poet has a vision of his father as a boy in Trigg County, Kentucky. The poet, in the autumn of his life, looks down the "tube and darkening corridor of

Time" and sees the youth "poised between woods and the pasture, sun-green and green shadow." Aware of what time holds in store for his father, the poet yearns to speak across the years: "Out of my knowl-edge, I would cry out and say: / *Listen!* Say: *Listen! I know—Oh I know—let me tell you!*" But the "hieratic" boy turns "with imperial calm" and reenters the shadow of the woods, confident of his own springtime promise.

In "Mortmain" the autobiographical element is very strong. The series is, Warren said, "clearly personal. Further, the personal urgen-cies are dramatized, are overtly presented, not merely absorbed."[4] In the voice of this new poetry there is a sudden sense of release, a quality of facility and amplitude lacking in the earlier work. The terms "open" and "confessional" poetry have never been very helpful, and insofar as they have come to mean the poetry of indiscretion or of expiation, they would be misleading if applied to Warren's verse. He is, the reader suspects, wary of the tendency of that verse toward moral posturing and self-absorption. But beginning with *Promises*, his poetry does have a greater "openness" in the sense that it is more revelatory and more accessible. The poems are, as Warren said in 1966, "a life record, and live their own life by that fact."[5]

During his years as a student at Vanderbilt, Warren once wrote to Allen Tate expressing his dissatisfaction with a meeting of Fugitives:

> As I expected, my poem Romance Macaber was rather poorly received by the majority of the members. "Morbid, affected, unconvincing" were among various criticisms applied. Hirsch with customary pomp inquired if the thing was not extremely personal; "the expression of an extremely personal passion and emotion, etc." I was compelled to reply that had it been I would never have read it to the company there assembled.

The letter indicates how far Warren has come from the objective, impersonal attitude toward poetry of his Fugitive days. The poetry after *Promises* speaks with "an extremely personal passion and emo-tion" and that is the chief source of its power.[6]

III Incarnations: Poems 1966–1968

After *You, Emperors, and Others* Warren waited six years before publishing a representative sampling of both the early and later verse, together with some new work, under the title *Selected Poems, Old and*

New, 1923–1966. He continued to write steadily—the poems coming in what he called "seizures"—and two years later he issued *Incarnations: Poems 1966–1968.* This new work explored fresh subject matter at the same time that it extended the boundaries of his art. Judging from the variety of reactions these poems evoked, or provoked, they left in their wake considerable confusion and bafflement.

One obvious characteristic of this new manner is the typography. Warren took great pains with the appearance of the poem on the page, adding a visual effect to all the other effects that poetry can produce. His public readings during the 1960s bore out this new concern. Before reading, he would hold up a typescript to the audience to let them see for themselves the arrangement of words on the page. The very extravagance of white space gives the poetry a portentousness lacking in a more traditional format. Confronted by only two lines on a single page, the reader feels compelled to linger over them. The problem arises when the lines fail to command the necessary scriptural power.

There is nothing new in this attention to typography. One thinks of the iconographic poets of the seventeenth century and, more recently, of the poems of E. E. Cummings. Here is an example from Warren's "A Problem in Spatial Composition":

> The hawk,
> Entering the composition at the upper left frame
> Of the window, glides,
> In the pellucid ease of thought and at
> His breathless angle.
> Down.
>
> Breaks speed.
>
> Hangs with a slight lift and hover.
>
> Makes contact.

The downward descent of the bird is recapitulated in the movement of the typography. The effect is entirely lost in oral presentation, and what is gained in silent reading, except a rather arch distraction, is debatable.

The typographical arrangement on the page is essentially a constituent of the rhythm. For Warren, rhythm—both in the strict sense of accent and in the broad sense of harmonic structure—is fundamental.

Speaking of rhythm, he has said: "In literature rhythm—not mere meter, but all the pulse of movement, density, and shadings of intensity of feeling—is the most intimate and compelling factor revealing to us the nature of the *thing made*."[7] The early poems are not metrically innovative, but achieve their effects within the traditional bounds of English prosody. The later poems, however, demonstrate a loosening of the line to the point where even Warren's most sympathetic readers complain that the effect is indistinguishable from prose—is, indeed, prosaic. The poem may appear to maintain a strict pattern on the page, but the lines seem arbitrary, broken more to satisfy the eye than to signify the sense.

An example of the problem is "Fall Comes to Back Country Vermont." A narrative of 120 lines, the poem compresses into one long, looping, convolved sentence a commentary on a village so small that a single death reduces the voter registration list to fifteen names. The reader scanning the very regular four-line stanzas on the page anticipates a metrically orthodox poem. Upon reading the poem, however, he finds that it violates all visual expectations, for the verse is neither regularly metrical nor accentual. The stanzaic pattern succeeds only in creating a false expectation. Consider the following stanza:

> Throw out from the car the empty bourbon
> Bottle to lie in the snow by the For-
> Sale sign, and snow covers the bottle, will cover
> The sign itself, and then the snow plow

The end of the line cannot resist an emphasis—it is irrevocably *there*. And so the reader asks: why separate "bourbon" from "bottle"? What is gained by the odd division of "For- Sale" other than a nagging distraction from the movement of the narrative? The experiment, in short, seems to create problems rather than to solve them.

All art is by nature deeply conservative. We read a new poem in the context of all the poems we have ever read. The satisfaction of art comes from the fashion in which the new work either satisfies an expectation or shocks us into new awareness. The problem with challenging a convention is that, in defying it, you acknowledge its existence and its power. In the case of stanzaic form, Warren's experiments suggest that, rather than turning the convention to his use, he is still in its thrall.

Another Warren experiment which yields mixed results is his tendency to conclude a poem with a prosaic assertion, usually abstract and often platitudinous. Consider the ending of "Shoes in Rain Jungle":

> This last is very important.

Or of "Riddle in the Garden":

> The world means only itself.

Or of "Deciduous Spring":

> There is something I am trying to remember.

In several poems this peculiar flatness becomes a principle of organization. "The Interim," one of a sequence called "Tale of Time," is such a poem. The stanzas of the poem characteristically begin with an abstract proposition, move to a series of concrete images, and conclude with another abstraction.

"Tell me what love is," section two begins, and ends, "You have not answered my question."

"There is only one solution," section six begins, and ends, "I would compare it with that fugitive thought which I can find no word for."

In this poem, and in others, Warren deliberately employs an antipoetic diction. For a writer so self-conscious, the flatness must be calculated, apparently to shock the reader into fresh consideration of the idea by the very triteness and clumsiness of the statement. Many of the poems seem, as well, tentative and inconclusive, as if the poet has chosen to carry on his search for his voice and style in public. What Warren said of Melville's poetry is equally true of his own: it "aims at the moment of poise, of synthesis, but . . . the poise and synthesis are hardwon, and often incomplete and provisional, and the awareness of that fact is the point, the 'truth' of the poetry."[8]

The best Warren poems in his new manner are those that come directly from his childhood and his family relationships, the personal emotion recollected in tranquility. The poems that deal with what might be called public topics—salesmen, Vietnam, penology—seem to be the least deeply felt, almost exercises. In form these new poems are chiefly lyric and dramatic. But Warren had not abandoned his old ambition to write a long historical narrative poem which would make a comprehensive statement about the human condition and reveal "the way life is."[9] After almost twenty years of reading, meditation, false starts, and blind alleys, he believed that he had finally found his subject in the career of Jean Jacques Audubon.

IV   Audubon: A Vision

Audubon: A Vision appeared in 1969 under circumstances which suggest the importance that Warren attached to it. Although running to about 440 lines and filling only thirty pages, the poem came out as a separate volume dedicated to his friend of Fugitive days and after, Allen Tate, and to Tate's wife Helen. The poem was heavily revised. Not a line, Warren said, existed in its original form.

Jean Jacques Audubon, the illegitimate son of a slave-trader in Santo Domingo, had the fantasist's gift of mythologizing his past. He was not, as some would have it, the Lost Dauphin of France, but was, as the poem says, "only himself." It is the special nature of that self which the poem seeks to encompass. Warren's treatment is extremely condensed. The verse varies from vivid, concrete narrative to cryptic and puzzling abstractions.

A reader picking up this slim volume might naturally expect it to deal with the famous paintings of the birds of America. Certainly Audubon the artist is central to Warren's conception, but the biographical incident that inspired the poem is of another order of interest, an act of random and inexplicable violence similar to that which drew him to the tales of Billie Potts and Lilburn Lewis.

Audubon, while traveling alone in the back country, seeks a night's lodging in the cabin of a slovenly frontier woman. When he carelessly reveals his gold pocket watch, the crone and her two hulking sons plot his murder. An Indian, also a seeker of shelter, warns Audubon of the plot against him. He awakens at night just as the sons are poised to attack and is miraculously saved by three men who at the crucial moment burst into the hovel. The following morning Audubon witnesses the hanging of the mother and the two sons.

This experience forms the heart of the poem, about half the lines, and it is told with extraordinary vividness and intensity. We meet Audubon standing alone in the forest. The poet, at first in a headnote and then in the opening lines, disabuses us at once of the more fantastic legends that have accreted about his hero. We then see Audubon (and the emphasis until the end is upon *vision*) observing the white heron and the bear with the inspired insight of the artist who created the great pictures. The special quality of Audubon's rendering is skillfully evoked. The point of view suddenly shifts from poet to subject and Audubon "thinks / How thin is the membrane between himself and the world." The irony is instantly apparent. His sense of his oneness with nature will soon be agonizingly tested in the cabin.

Coming upon the cabin "like a wound rubbed raw in the vast pelt of the forest," he is fascinated by the half-savage woman:

> The face, in the air, hangs. Large,
> Raw-hewn, strong-beaked, the haired mole
> Near the nose, to the left, and the left side by firelight
> Glazed red, the right in shadow, and under the tumble and tangle
> Of dark hair on that head, and under the coarse eyebrows,
> The eyes, dark, glint as from the unspecifiable
> Darkness of a cave. It is a woman.

The narrative that follows is specific and relentless. Audubon is caught up in the forces which collectively are his fate, and, as Warren characterizes him, suffers a peculiar paralysis of will as the executioners approach. The following morning at the hanging he stares hypnotically at the face of the frontier crone. He cannot tear his eyes away.

>   The face,
> Eyes a-glare, jaws clenched, now glowing black with congestion
> Like a plum, had achieved,
> It seemed to him, a new dimension of beauty.

Experiencing an epiphany, he is moved both sexually and spiritually by the event.

The consequence for Audubon is that he discovers, or stumbles upon, the quality that Warren heroes forever seek—identity. Like "definition," identity is one of the mystic words for Warren—cabalistic, personal, central. The remainder of the poem is a kind of collage of quotations from Audubon's works, apostrophes by the poet, and cryptic and haunting images of the natural world. They blend into a celebration of "blessedness." That state can only be contemplated, not communicated, but the poem gallantly attempts to find the correlative for the experience.

In the closing sequence the poet, turning suddenly autobiographical, speaks of his own boyhood in Kentucky. He stands in the darkness and hears the geese flying northward (one can only guess at the personal significance of *north* in this context). Significantly he hears, but he cannot see. Then he turns from the birds, the objects seen so clearly by Audubon in his art, to the art that has preoccupied Warren for a lifetime. "Tell me a story," the poet says. "Tell me a story of deep delight."

Scholars have already set to work to demonstrate that the Audubon who lives in Warren's poem is "unhistorical." The places where he varies from his source, the five-volume *Ornithological Biography*, are obvious, their significance much less so. Certainly it is idle to fault him on minor inconsistencies when his professed interest is in what he likes to call the "inwardness" of the human situation. Warren's attitude toward the past is, one suspects, similar to the attitude he assigns to Hawthorne: "What Hawthorne found in the past was not the quaint charm of distance but the living issues of moral psychological definition. What the fact of the past gave him was a distancing of the subject to gain an archetypal clarity and mythic force."[10]

Audubon: A Vision is unique among Warren's works. Nowhere else are his characteristic themes and techniques presented in a more condensed form. Everything is here: the fascination with violence, the sense of history, the need to know, the obsession with identity, the yearning for serenity. And the themes are treated in the blend of frontier colloquial and high literary which is the Warren signature.

Admirers of Warren will tend to overvalue *Audubon* simply because it is such a distillation of all that is typical in his work. Those admirers cannot overlook the blemishes that are equally typical—the elliptical quality carried to extremes, the occasional pretentiousness, and the abstraction which, depending on the reader's mood, strikes him as either profound or preposterous. *Audubon: A Vision* is *the* Warren poem, the inevitable choice for the anthologist in search of the representative selection from his work.

V   Or Else: Poem/Poems

Five years separates *Audubon: A Vision* from *Or Else: Poem/ Poems 1968–1974*. The poems included in the new volume have a rather tangled history extending back over fifteen years. In a headnote Warren remarks that in the late 1950s he began working toward a long poem. "After a time," he wrote, "I was to find that the poem was disintegrating into a miscellany, and so abandoned the project." Ten of these pieces he placed at the opening of *Selected Poems 1923–1966* under the title "Notes on a Life to Be Lived." Two more poems were later incorporated into *Incarnations* (1968) under the title "The True Nature of Time." Finally, he decided that "Homage to Theodore Dreiser," the elegy he had placed at the front of his study of the novelist, had a place in the thematic structure of the long poem.

Thus the history of the composition of *Or Else* suggests that it had been long meditated by its author and that its materials, while obviously of compelling personal significance, proved to be particularly intractable. The note of indecision in the book's subtitle, *Poem/Poems*, calls attention to his ambivalence about the ultimate coherence of the total work. And, as Warren explained, the dates which presumably bracket the volume, *1968–1974*, are not intended to be taken literally.

The poem is divided into twenty-four parts. Within this structure there are eight intercalary poems each numbered and labeled "Interjection," as if to point up the underlying unity of the poem as a whole. These interruptions, often gnomic and speculative, enhance, by a kind of counterpoint, the lyricism of the total work.

Or Else makes a stately progress through a variety of modes—lyric, elegiac, narrative, aphoristic. The development is not chronological, but rather the narrator ranges freely backward and forward in time as he turns once again to images in his memory which persist and cry out for interpretation. A small white house "swims in the dazzle of no-Time." A "beat-up old" 1931 Studebaker moves "like a dot into / distance trailing its red plume of / dust toward the horizon." In a meadow in Wyoming framed by mountains, a little boy loses his shoe in a field and hobbles home, aimlessly whipping the goldenrod with a stick. The images pile up, but the narrator wonders if they add up. He says, "I have now put on record one thing that is not important but simply is." At the conclusion of another story, the narrator confesses, "All I can do is to offer my testimony." This ransacking of the past leads him ultimately to an overwhelming question: "Have I learned how to live?"

In its range and in its insistent probing, *Or Else* attempts to provide an answer to that question. Most of the preoccupations that have concerned Warren, have indeed obsessed him, throughout his long career all find a place. The poem is, in fact, so comprehensive that all Warren's work constitutes a gloss on it.

The volume contains several long set pieces, variations on the theme

of the literary life. "Flaubert in Egypt" is an exercise in eroticism. The
most ambitious, that on Theodore Dreiser, is also the most conventional
in form. The most obviously personal is "Folly on Royal Street," a
funny reminiscence of three aesthetes on a dull Sunday morning in
New Orleans. The three friends are very young, very broke, and very
drunk. The years have passed and the lives of the other two seem now
to the speaker baffling and inconclusive. Of himself he says:

> As for the third, the tale
> Is short. But long,
> How long the art, and wisdom slow!

Or Else can also be read as a Warren anthology. "Ballad of Mister
Dutcher and the Last Lynching in Gupton" is another of his terse,
powerful narratives. The "Ballad," like the earlier "Court-martial" or
the still earlier "Ballad of Billie Potts," is in a genre which Warren has
made distinctively his own. The effect comes from the rigorous economy and the narrative drive, but also from the diction, an amalgam of
regional colloquial, bemused irony, and literary allusion.

"News Photo" is a counterpart to the "Ballad." The theme is the
same, the violence bred by racial hatred, but this time the action is set
a generation later. The narrator, studying the photograph of a man
emerging from a court room after being acquitted of murdering a
political agitator, is led to speculate on the generations of bigotry
behind him. Over the scene broods the ghostly presence of Robert E.
Lee. The poem dramatizes the theme that has always attracted Warren
and that was given most explicit statement in his essay *Segregation*:
the conflicting demands of generational piety in the South.

Examples of the cumulative interest of *Or Else* for the longtime
admirer of Warren are everywhere. But for the reader particularly
drawn to the achievement of the last twenty years, the theme that
emerges with greatest force, in fact as the organizing principle of the
work, is the relationship of child to parent, the vexing blend of affection, resentment, and guilt which over the years has resisted definition.

The theme is announced at once in "Natural History," a delightfully
surrealist vision of a "naked old" father cavorting in the rain and a
"naked old" mother madly counting her money. The poem has the
bizarre and dimly perceived symbolism of a dream. The speaker
resents the parents' implied demand that he attend to them, that he
try to understand what they are saying to him so obliquely. "They

must learn to stay in their graves," he says. "That is what graves are for." His tone, however, is ironic, for he knows that their claims are inescapable.

This theme of the claims of the dead parents on the living poet is realized with great vividness in the longest poem in the collection, "I Am Dreaming of a White Christmas." Like all artists Warren is better when he reveals than when he expounds, and in this poem he has created a memorable image for the hold of the past upon the present. The speaker remembers a Christmas morning in his youth and speculates about the contents of three identical boxes wrapped and set under the tree for him, his sister, and the baby. For the speaker, Time has stopped but not its processes. Even memory cannot arrest the inexorable decay. The figures of his parents, the furniture, the room are all hideously decomposed and covered with "That silken and yellow perfection of Time that / Dust is. . . ." The eye sockets of his father stare blindly. From the holes in the skull, "Deep and dark as a thumb gouge," the narrator sees

> Something that might be taken for
> A mulberry, large and black-ripe when, long back, crushed,
> But now, with years, dust-dried. The mulberries
> Crushed and desicated, each out of
> Its dark lurking-place, stare out at
> Nothing.
>
> >His eyes
> Had been blue.

Turning to the mother, he sees her sitting in her accustomed rocker, but now her leg bone thrusts through the frayed and tattered skirt. The poem captures the blend of the poet's fascination and horror, his natural revulsion from the scene coupled with his compulsion to dwell on each macabre detail.

Abruptly the narrator is recalled to the present. He stands in Times Square and catalogs the inevitable details of the wasteland, equally hideous and equally doomed: the "hysteria of neon," and the blunt crowd that "thrusts, nudges, jerks, jostles. . . ." The concluding stanza could stand as the epigraph for the entire volume:

> All items listed above belong in the world
> In which all things are continuous,

And are parts of the original dream which
I am now trying to discover the logic of. This
Is the process whereby pain of the past in its pastness
May be converted into the future tense

Of joy.

These poems appearing early in the book foreshadow the penultimate section of *Or Else* in which the poet, in an elegiac mood, turns
again to the relationship of parent and child. "There's a Grandfather's
Clock in the Hall" collects images out of memory, trying to sort them
into some pattern of meaning. The speaker wishes to recapture the
semblance of the past, but it is in his own timebound consciousness and
his memories that he must look for it. What he seems only dimly to
perceive is that his preoccupation with self and his vanity are the chief
impediments to self-knowledge. A chain of free association carries the
narrator from a haunted and time-obsessed life to the bedside of his
dying mother. The emotions he experiences—physical disgust, impa-
tience, hatred—are the reverse of the conventional ones he might be
expected to anticipate and to celebrate. The mother asks a question of
"murderous triviality"—providing another soul-destroying memory
for the speaker—and in that moment "Time / thrusts through the time
/ of no-Time."

"Reading Late at Night, Thermometer Falling," an elegy on the
dead father, makes explicit the fact that the poet is returning to the
subject:

          So, Sir, I
Who certainly could never have addressed you on a matter
As important as this when you were not dead, now
Address you on it for the last time, even though
Not being, after all my previous and sometimes desperate efforts,
Sure what a son can ever say to a father, even
A dead one.

Twelve years earlier Warren had attempted the same subject in "Mortmain." He had been sufficiently satisfied with the result to select it for
an anthology, *Poet's Choice*, in which poets were asked to choose their
own favorites from among their works.[11] Many of his readers would
probably have agreed that it represented the best of his new work. And
"Mortmain" remains a fine performance. But it is instructive to com-

pare it with "Reading Late at Night, Thermometer Falling." The earlier poem seems by comparison abstract and convoluted, heavy with speculation and elaboration. The new poem is a character study, less cluttered, more dramatic, a narrative which gains its power from the starkness of the diction and the simplicity of its presentation. The father is allowed to dominate the scene and to speak for himself. The poem rises to an eloquent climax in the vision of the past, a massive glacier, grinding imperceptibly but inexorably. The later poem is less self-conscious and consequently more sincere. The voice of the poet is easy, assured, and authoritative.

The personal, familiar poems collected in *Or Else* represent a natural fulfillment of the themes first shadowed forth in *Promises*. With great subtlety these verses preserve the precious and baffling moments that seem to embody and to reveal a truth. The narrator, while his experience parallels that of Warren, is nevertheless a fictional construct, an Everyman. His goal is self-definition—to discover himself in the process of becoming himself. Readers who complained of overwriting, of self-parody, of events insufficiently dramatized in the previous work will find less in *Or Else* to displease them. Uneven, as much of the later work is, *Or Else* is the volume in which Warren's special poetic gifts are most fully realized.

CHAPTER 7

Tennessee Pastoral

THE enthusiastic reception given to Warren's new poetry consolidated his position on the American literary scene, and he began at last to receive the kind of public recognition that had always eluded him. The Pulitzer Prize for *Promises* in 1957 was his second, making him the only writer to have won the award for both fiction and poetry. In the intervening years he has carried off most of the honors in the field: among them the Bollingen Prize, the National Medal for Literature, the Van Wyck Brooks Award, the Copernicus Prize, the Emerson-Thoreau Award, and the Harriet Monroe Prize. Inevitably, the honorary degrees and the memberships in honorary societies have followed.

Warren's versatility is unique and extraordinary. One reviewer, noting his contribution to fiction, poetry, drama, criticism, and biography, called him the "pentathlon champion" of American literature. To that list must be added social commentary. For with fame came the invitations to contribute to the insatiable national appetite for punditry. In 1961 *Life* magazine asked him to write something on the Civil War, and the piece overflowed into a long essay, *The Legacy of the Civil War*, which was published separately to wide acclaim. In 1965 he contributed to the national dialogue on the problem of race relations with a volume of interviews he conducted with leaders of the black community—*Who Speaks for the Negro?* Praised for its balance and sanity, it remains a significant document in that continuing national debate.

A reticent and self-effacing man, Warren affected neither the eccentricity nor the flamboyance that might have endeared him to the mass media. He and his wife, Eleanor Clark, and their two children live in Fairfield, Connecticut, breaking the rhythm of their lives there with summers in West Wardsboro, Vermont. The family went to Europe for extended stays which Warren enjoyed, feeling that the "foreignness" of the experience turned him back on his own language in ways valuable to an artist. Fairfield is close to New Haven, and one semester a year until his retirement in 1973 he taught what he calls "the finest flower of Yale literarydom."[1]

I *Warren as an Academic*

The anonymity that he seems to have cultivated does not carry over into academic life. His novels, especially *All the King's Men*, are taught in modern literature classes and his poetry is represented in the anthologies. But it is through his textbooks that he is best known to two generations of college students and their professors. In 1938 he collaborated with Cleanth Brooks on *Understanding Poetry*, a textbook designed to recall professors and students from peripheral concerns to the actual subject of their study—the poem itself. Organizing and simplifying a wide variety of critical ideas just coming into favor, the book and two later revisions swept the country's English departments and dominated literary study in the United States at least until the 1960s.

In the period immediately before World War I a number of literary critics, in reaction to the dominance of literary history and of "appreciation," had been insisting on a greater attention to the text, on an increased awareness of irony and ambiguity. These practitioners of "close reading," although their individual styles and viewpoints varied widely, had been loosely grouped together as practitioners of a New Criticism. *Understanding Poetry*, systematizing the insights of many of these critics into a method with its own jargon, in effect institutionalized the New Criticism. The result was revolutionary. On campus in those days no reference to "Marx and Engels" or to "Freud and Jung" carried any more weight than an appeal to "Brooks and Warren." The staid author of a weighty chapter on recent literary history, recalling the joy as an undergraduate of discovering the new textbook, was moved to quote Wordsworth: "Bliss was it in that dawn to be alive. . . ."[2]

Warren's own career in academe kept pace with the success of *Understanding Poetry* and the texts and anthologies that followed it. His teaching appointments are a model of upward mobility: Southwestern, Vanderbilt, Louisiana State, Minnesota, Yale. Yet he seems in later years to have been ambivalent about academic life. Three times he quit teaching, only to return, acknowledging, as did Randall Jarrell, that he would gladly pay for the privilege. But despite the claims of the classroom, the books continued to appear at an undiminished rate.

II   The Cave

Warren surprised those who predicted that *Promises* meant he was abandoning prose fiction by bringing out two years later, in 1959, a novel entitled *The Cave*. After his long immersion in American history, he gave this new novel a contemporary setting. The time is the spring of 1955 and the place is a world already explored in *At Heaven's Gate*: a large southern city and a small rural town in Tennessee. The genesis of the story was an actual event.

In January 1925 Warren, then a senior at Vanderbilt, watched with the rest of the country the tragedy of Floyd Collins trapped in nearby Sand Cave, Kentucky. Young Collins was exploring an underground passage near Mammoth Cave in search of something to attract tourists when a large stone became dislodged, pinning his foot. An enterprising reporter for a Louisville newspaper slithered through the slime to interview Collins. The reports from the scene caught the national fancy, and a barrage of headlines and bulletins kept the public in a state of suspense concerning Collins's plight. Within two weeks a tent city had sprung up near the cave mouth, and milling crowds had to be restrained by state troopers with drawn bayonets. Since Collins could not be reached through the cave passage, an effort was made to cut a shaft from outside. When on the eighteenth day he was found dead, his body was sealed in the cave and funeral services were held on the hill above. This event provided a dramatic instance of the power of the mass media to stir the populace by an assault on their emotions. Within a month a North Carolina cave-in caught seventy-one men and fifty-three were killed. "It attracted," Frederick Lewis Allen observed drily, "no great notice."[3]

The Cave centers on an incident similar to the Collins story. The action traces three days in the life of Johntown—the involvement of a dozen or so townsfolk in the suffering of a "cave crawler," Jasper Harrick, and the cynical exploitation of that suffering by the "Big Media."

Warren controls and formalizes his materials in *The Cave* by employing a shifting angle of vision which reduces the need for authorial commentary. The action rendered symbolically is itself an interpretation. The central event of the novel, a young man trapped in a cave, is refracted through the consciousness of each of a group of very limited and imperfect human beings: people trapped by their narrowness of self, who convey their perceptions and sensations in a language suited to their backgrounds and experience. The variety of voices made possible a broad range of styles and released Warren's gift for earthy and often ribald humor which had been seldom in evidence since *All the King's Men*.

The characters of *The Cave* have, in several instances, the familiarity of people already encountered in Warren's fiction. Jack Harrick, "old heller of high coves and hoot-owl hollows," like Sergeant Alvin York of Pall Mall, Tennessee, is a country blacksmith who won the Congressional Medal of Honor in France. Although Warren had already drawn such a figure in Private Porsum of *At Heaven's Gate*, he makes Harrick an older Porsum, more fully realized than the dim and insubstantial character of the earlier work. Like Porsum, Harrick is a hillbilly, extraordinarily gifted with a rifle and a "sleight for cover," but is first baffled and then victimized by his heroism and its consequences. Betrayed by an overweening faith in his physical vitality, he is dying of cancer and can find small spiritual comfort from his conversion to Christianity. Jack's son Jasper is also a war hero, having distinguished himself in Korea. He is another familiar figure in the Warren canon—Captain Todd in *Night Rider* is an example, as is Miss Idell of *Band of Angels*—a person blessed with a certainty of self which is the envy and despair of those around him: "He had that trick of being himself so completely, it looked like he wore the whole world over his shoulders like a coat" (19). The source of Jasper's confidence remains a mystery, for he is the only major character into whose consciousness we do not enter.

Jack Harrick's boyhood friend, the Reverend MacCarland Sumpter, is a kind of first cousin to the Scholarly Attorney in *All the King's Men*. Each, having faced the truth that his wife has carried the child of another man, sublimates that knowledge into a dogged, fanatic faith. Both are driven by the fear that their faith may prove under stress to be built on sand. Each has reared a boy whom he believes to be cynical and irreverent. Sumpter's son, Isaac, shares with Jack Burden a rather sophomoric cynicism and a wise-cracking style compounded of slang and profanity interlarded with literary allusions. There is something, too, of Jerry Calhoun in Isaac Sumpter, for both have about them the smell of success, both are untroubled by self-knowledge, and both are lost.

To point up these similarities to earlier characters is not to suggest a descent into redundancy but to insist on the consistency of the line of Warren's artistic development. In fact, the novel contains a gallery of diverse and freshly observed characters. One of these is "the Greek," Nicholas Papadoupalous, for whom Johntown is the latest in a list of failures southward: Cincinnati, Louisville, Nashville. Nick—physically powerful, suspicious, unlucky, and stupid—impetuously marries a dancer in a burlesque show because she reminds him of Jean Harlow, the movie queen of the 1930s. Now, however, she is dying slowly and expensively of tuberculosis, and Nick is deeply in debt to the Johntown bank. Its president, Timothy Bingham—cowardly, self-doubting, ineffectual—represents together with his wife, Matilda, the gentility of Johntown. Their marriage, a misalliance, reaches its crisis with the discovery that their only daughter, Jo-Lea, is pregnant with the child of Jack Harrick's younger son, Monty.

The novel's epigraph, drawn from the Allegory of the Cave, gives us the first clue to its meaning. The story is one of the most famous passages in Plato's *Republic*. The inhabitants of a cave have been obliged to live out their lives chained with their backs to the mouth of the cave, unable to see the light of truth burning above and behind them. Knowing only the shadows cast on the wall at the rear of the cave and mistaking the echoes from the wall for the source of the sounds they hear, they accept the shadowy illusion for the reality they cannot know. Even if they were unshackled from their chains and forced to contemplate the light, they would find it distressing and painful. Only by being dragged reluctantly to the mouth of the cave could they be persuaded that their familiar world of shadows is not real and that the brilliant light outside is not merely a brighter illusion. It is just such a cave that Warren shows us in his novel. Each character is committed to his own version of a shadow world and, in being compelled by circumstances to face reality, each must leave the dark cavern of his own nature to face the light of self-knowledge. For Isaac Sumpter, the knowledge of self is too painful to accept, and he clings to the familiar illusory world. For others, emergence is a kind of rebirth, a recognition and acceptance of the essential self.

Warren has adapted Plato's basic metaphor and used it with countless variations for his own purposes. Characters are repeatedly shown in deep shadow, squinting into the brilliance outside and failing to grasp the implications of what they see. An example is the idle speculations of Jack Harrick's wife, Celia: "She kept . . . looking out from the shadow of the hall, then out under the deepening shadow of the maple boughs in the yard and the big cedars, out into the open where the light lay so sweet and far away like a place she would never come again" (290). Again, at the climax of the novel: "Jack Harrick had to force himself to face the open door, where the shadows of the hall piled up. Then he saw the figure appear in the space. The face, white against the shadows, was the face of MacCarland Sumpter" (377).

The patterns of imagery of the novel reinforce and elaborate the symbolism of the cave. Jack Harrick, troubled by a vague disquietude, contemplates the "big black hole right in the middle of him where a man's thinking and feeling and living ought to be" (139). When he meets the woman he will marry, Celia Hornby, he tells her: "I bet if I threw a rock down your well, I'd be listening down in the dark a long time before it hit water" (168). Monty Harrick, in the early days of his courtship of Jo-Lea Bingham, had not allowed her "to enter the dark-ened room of his fantasy" (8). Nicholas Papadoupalous broods on his repeated failures "in the deep, dark, angry, tear-sodden secret center of his being" (41). MacCarland Sumpter, lamenting his wife's death in childbirth, felt "as though a level of black water rose from the floor to overwhelm him" (83).

The shadow of Sigmund Freud falls across the novel for the cave symbolism has the particular connotations of womb and tomb which Freudian theory has taught us to attach to it. The cave is, literally, the tomb of Jasper Harrick; and Isaac Sumpter is overcome with envy for him "because he lay in the cool, cool dark and did not suffer" (324). Warren depicts the consequences of the longing for withdrawal and nonbeing in nightmare images of claustrophobic terror. Isaac Sumpter, fearful that his privacy has been breached, feels a "sudden terror at being spied on, as though he were spinning away, down and down, into the depths of an astronomical telescope" (104). And then there is the cry of Miss Abernathy, confessing publicly that she has sinned car-nally with Jack Harrick: "It was a thin, wailing cry of lostness, like somebody falling down a well, a well infinitely deep" (321).

The cave is also a womblike retreat where Jasper can "lie snug and complete with the whole world tucked in around him" (19). The cave as womb symbol functions on another level as an aspect of the theme of rebirth. Isaac Sumpter, entering the cave to search for Jasper, senses a new confidence stirring within himself and formulates this feeling in imagery reminiscent of the rebirth motif in *All the King's Men*:

. . . his self was the self that knew that this being now stirred in the dew-darkness. But it had to be a self, for it was contained in the darkness which was himself. It was, he knew in a knowledge that was not quite knowledge, at least not quite words, a self of the self, a free, immortal self, ready for song, being born this instant in the darkness of the self that suffered and was free. (99)

Related to the concept of the cave as womb symbol is Warren's reliance on sexual motivation in the delineation of character. He has given us an exhaustive and explicit account of the sex lives of the people of Johntown. There are the fantasies of Nicholas Papadoupalous, the deprivations of Timothy Bingham, and the "absoluteness and animality" of Isaac Sumpter. Jack Harrick catalogues his epic fornications in the closing pages of the novel until it seems a man's life consists in the number of women he possesses. What gives these scenes of sexuality their particular horror is not so much the coarse language in which they are described as the lack of any degree of human warmth in them. Sex is either a form of coldly egotistical aggression or a violent and mechanical coupling. The cave of sexuality, like the cave of illusion, reverberates hollowly.

Ironically, these people are using sex as a proclamation of self. Crippled emotionally by blunted sensibilities and plodding minds, they are nevertheless groping confusedly in the shadows, searching for some light of truth, and as usual in Warren's work, the search for truth begins with the search for identity. To dramatize the blurring of identity in his characters, Warren has elaborated a technique he has used before: the multiplying of names for his characters to suggest the variety of masks with which they face the world. Jack Harrick is "Jumping Jack" to his buddies in the United States Army, a sexual athlete and a slaughterer of the Hun. To his wife, twenty-five years his junior, he is "John T.," for she finds in his masculinity a symbol of dominance she never found in her father. To the hillbillies, he is "Old Jack," an almost mythic figure. Isaac Sumpter, when living parasitically with a wealthy co-ed at the university, Rachel Goldstein, nicknames her, significantly enough, "Goldie." Later, when she is only a projection of his own self-esteem, she is simply generalized into the "Jew Girl." His own shifting sense of identity is betrayed when, in signing either his love letters or his by-line for the press, he hesitates craftily between "Isaac" and "Ikey." Nicholas Papadoupalous, estranged by his foreignness in xenophobic Johntown, cannot find a single citizen in the county who can pronounce his name correctly. His wife, Sarah Pumfret, has taken the stage name of Giselle Fontaine, but to her husband she is, at least in fantasy, Jean Harlow.

The Cave is a story of communal guilt, for, as MacCarland Sumpter points out, Jasper Harrick is reenacting the plight of each man trapped in the darkness which is himself. Every man is diminished by the death of Jasper, and this ebbing of vitality is symbolized in the novel by the recurring image of bleeding. Nicholas Papadoupalous, his world slipping out of control, "felt like he was bleeding away in weakness" (267). Celia Harrick feels a sense of defraudment, "like a tiny wound bleeding its single silky thread of blood on her white skin" (294). Isaac Sumpter's vague stirrings of discontent are "like a tiny ulcer in his brain, unhealing forever and oozing" (366).

These examples, only a few of the many possible, suggest the symbolic richness of *The Cave*. At times, however, the very profusion of imagery seems a mechanical and calculated intrusion rather than an integral part of the action. The conclusion of the novel, a series of epiphanies in which the central characters achieve a measure of serenity and self-knowledge, seems forced and gratuitous. Jack Harrick's final insight—"I reckon living is just learning how to die. And . . . dying [is] just learning how to live"—comes with the thud of anticlimax. As a study of limited and very human people who find themselves inadequate to the demands of a complex and value-stripped society, *The Cave* is a solid, moving performance. As a study of rebirth and renewal, it is unconvincing, for the artificiality of the ending seriously mars the total effect of the work. Warren's readiness to resolve the conflicts of a varied and benighted cast of characters demands a suspension of disbelief greater than many readers will be able to summon.

The Cave received a respectful but lukewarm reception from the critical press when it appeared in 1959. Two years later *Wilderness*, discussed earlier in connection with Warren's historical fiction, was also something of a critical disappointment, although its reception was tempered by the climate of enthusiasm created by the onset of the Civil War Centennial. Warren's next novel, *Flood: A Romance of Our Time*, appeared in 1964 and was promptly savaged.

III   Flood: A Romance of Our Time

Every once in a while a novel will appear and provoke among its reviewers contempt, and even fury, out of all proportion to its alleged defects. What calls out such a response is something of a mystery. Why should a novel—an illusion aspiring to pass for a reality—precipitate such a tantrum in the reviewer? Perhaps he had predicted great prom-

ise for the author and is outraged at being proved a false prophet. Or
perhaps he envies a large reputation, for a merciless drubbing is seldom
wasted on a first novel but is reserved for a larger target. Whatever the
reason, literary history offers a number of examples of such massacres.
Ernest Hemingway's *Across the River and Into the Trees* is one
instance and Thomas Wolfe's *From Death to Morning* is another.

The news magazines, as usual, were the first to report, and the news
was devastating. *Newsweek* thought *Flood* "one of the worst books by
a good writer ever to appear," and *Time* denounced it as an "emotionally besotted verbal debauch." With characteristic archness, the
New Yorker found it "rough hewn from blocks of marshmallow."[4] The
academic establishment was hostile and even the journals from Warren
country—the *Virginia Quarterly Review* and the *Sewannee Review*—
were tepid.

It would be pleasant to record that the howling tribe of reviewers
was made up of myopic brutes, that *Flood* is in fact a work of subtlety
and power too rare for Grub Street, that it is one of those ground-
breaking books that must create its own audience. It is not. *Flood* still
reads like a parody, if not of William Faulkner as many of its early
readers believed, then of Warren himself. In perspective it seems more
and more like the death knell of the Southern School, the ultimate
anthology of decayed aristocracy, blood taint, miscegenation, hapless
chivalry, and lost causes. The reader meets yet again the swamp rat,
the hip young black, the sex-starved old maid, the bluff country squire
with a mulatto mistress, and the half-crazed old lady lurking in dim
hallways of a decrepit mansion.

Flood is, moreover, an irritating book. But it does not irritate in a
way to shock or goad the reader into fresh perceptions. Rather, *Flood*
is irritating in a way that makes the reader suspect its sincerity. It does
not ring true. The reasons are worth searching out, for the failures of
the gifted can be as interesting and as instructive as their triumphs.

The world of *Flood* is the world of Middle Tennessee already made
familiar to us in *At Heaven's Gate, The Cave,* and in many poems
since *Promises.* The federal government is building a dam which will
flood the decaying town of Fiddlersburg. Attracted by the cinematic
possiblities of the incident, two men, each in his own way a celebrity,
come to Fiddlersburg to make a motion picture. One, Yasha Jones, is
a Hollywood director. The other, Bradwell Tolliver, is a successful
screen writer. Yasha Jones is an exotic, an intellectual carpetbagger
who will exploit the dispossessed. Bradwell Tolliver is a native son of

Fiddlersburg, obsessed with the need to demonstrate that you can go home again.

The novel is not so much about what happens to Bradwell Tolliver, although a good deal does happen to him, as it is about what happens to the inhabitants of the town, those who never left home, as a consequence of his return. The reader discovers as the story unfolds that this is Bradwell Tolliver's second return home. The events of this second journey resemble the first to the point of *déjà vu* and are about equally disastrous for all concerned. Bradwell Tolliver is a destroyer, not by calculation or for vengeance, but through some poisonous and anarchic streak in his twisted nature.

From the tangled skein of the narrative the life of Bradwell Tolliver, equally tangled, begins to emerge. The first stage begins with the boyhood in Fiddlersburg with the friend of his youth, Calvin Fiddler, scion of the town's first family. It draws to an end with a stay at Darthurst College and the publication of a precocious collection of short stories.

In the second stage, Bradwell fights in the Spanish Civil War, is disillusioned by politics, and brings a new wife, Lettice Poindexter, back to Fiddlersburg to find his roots and to make a new start. Lettice is a familiar Warren type: the limber-legged, high-bosomed fantasy figure (Lois in *All the King's Men* is another) who willingly and selflessly provides spectacular sex on demand. Bradwell's rural idyll with Lettice comes apart when Calvin Fiddler, now a Johns Hopkins general practitioner married to Bradwell's younger sister, Maggie, discovers her infidelity and murders her lover, Alfred O. Tuttle, "the Tuttle boy," the innocent interloper and victim.

The novel opens as the third stage begins. Calvin Fiddler has been in the Fiddlersburg penitentiary for almost twenty years; his wife, Maggie, has been living in seclusion with her mother-in-law, and the waters are about to rise. There follows a series of improbable and melodramatic events—a love affair between Maggie and Yasha Jones, a prison break by Calvin, the seduction of a blind girl by Bradwell, and his beating at the hands of a black gas station attendant who studied Romance languages at the University of Chicago.

Such a summary not only falsifies the novel more than most plot summaries do but also does an injustice to the formal design of *Flood*. Over the years Warren has lost none of his fascination with the idea of Time, with the way we experience it and transmute it into History. In *Flood* he turns to the peculiar doubleness of the life of the artist: his life in time and his work out of time. The novel is about this struggle:

to live life or to immortalize it. It is, as well, about the shadowy half-world where the raw materials of experience are transformed into the constructs of art.

In its intricate flashbacks, its shifting points of view, its jarring and occasionally bewildering juxtapositions, its meditations by an omniscient narrator, *Flood* represents Warren's most ambitious attempt to dramatize the actual impingement of time on the human sensibility. The method works. The narrative deals subtly with both reminiscence and direct experience, with the gradual emergence of suppressed memories, and with the shock of revelation. Structurally, *Flood* is brilliant, the work of a master fictional strategist. The disappointment of the novel lies in its texture, in the garrulity of its style, and in the turgidity of its ideas.

Flood is the only Warren novel which is directly about the life of the artist in America. With his characteristic interest in the "doubleness of life," Warren creates two artists who represent contrasting views of their task. Yasha Jones is a self-dramatist and a poseur. With his studied sentences and his remote manner, he is too guarded to be either known or especially liked. He worries about the corruption of consciousness, worships authenticity, and distrusts formalism. "It is life that is so plotty," Yasha says. He is more the sensitive and intuitive aesthete. Speaking of the moving picture they will make together, he tells Bradwell Tolliver, "We want a flow of feeling."

Yasha Jones takes himself seriously as befits a boy wonder of Hollywood. He is given such speeches as, "You might say science is the right telling. And that art is the right not-telling" (118). He is apparently intended to be the artist as romantic man of action, the esthete who will make his life a work of art, realizing it "in time." As a character in fiction Yasha Jones provides a necessary angle in the geometry of the novel, but Warren seems ultimately rather bored with him. Or perhaps, he is interested in scoring a few points on a type he doesn't especially like.

Much care, however, is lavished on Bradwell Tolliver, whose artistic career bears a number of parallels to that of his creator. Like Tolliver, Warren left the South but continued to return to it and to exploit it for his artistic purposes. And like his hero, Warren wrote a famous story in 1946, then tried his hand at screen writing, even winning an award for it. The peculiar ambivalence Bradwell Tolliver feels for his native region is, as we have seen, a major theme and central tension in Warren's work. The parallel between Tolliver and Warren, however, is not to be insisted upon.

Bradwell Tolliver is infected with the yen for literary immortality. His first and only genuine achievement came with a book of short stories written about Fiddlersburg while he was still in college, and his work since as a screen writer he correctly believes to be bogus, a sellout. He believes, or says he believes, that "when you are writing a story or doing a movie script, you hit some logic and it is that logic, not the heart business, that drives you to a certain end" (231). In Fiddlersburg he hopes to recapture his first inspiration, but he has trouble detaching himself from his subject matter, and he has learned to distrust his emotions. In fact, alternately awash in whisky and self-pity, he has difficulty summoning up any emotion at all.

As an artist, Bradwell Tolliver's chief problem is that he is a wretched self-critic, particularly of his own humor. Both insistent and insensitive, he is the sort of person who thinks it is funny to rechristen a Tennessee Williams play "Cat in the Hot Tin Pants" or to say devastating things about the Nashville Junior Chamber of Commerce. Bradwell is, in short, a bore. His tiresomeness stems largely from his inability to leave anything unsaid. This habit shows itself particularly when he is sniffing out the significance of things. We are introduced to the deputy warden of the Fiddlersburg penitentiary, Mr. Budd. His past as a heavyweight fighter and paratrooper has not unfitted him for a life of speculation. If we miss his point on loneliness in the penitentiary and the symbolic value of solitary confinement, Bradwell Tolliver drives it home in the next chapter. "Your philosophic friend Mr. Budd is right," he tells Yasha Jones. "It is the lonesomeness. The only reason everybody in Fiddlersburg does not get himself in the pen out of lonesomeness is because Fiddlersburg is a kind of pen already. . . . the whole South is lonesome" (165).

The narrative is lumpy with such unassimilated ideas. The idea of the "true lie," a concept Warren learned from Joseph Conrad and developed with subtlety and a fine sense of inevitability in *All the King's Men*, is stated baldly in *Flood*. "Yes," the narrator says, "reality was uncapturable. That was why we need illusion. *Truth through lie*, he thought" (50). Thrust out at us in italics, the phrase lacks dramatic context and, thus, either force or conviction. What Warren has said of Theodore Dreiser could also be said of him: "Dreiser's mind moved more and more toward generalization and abstraction, and . . . all the unfriendly criticism of Dreiser as an intellectual becomes more and more to the point."[5]

The Warren style has become more pronounced, more idiosyncratic, and more self-indulgent. There are the repetitions, the one-sentence

paragraphs, and the italicized thoughts. The allusiveness, once a part
of the action, is now often mere sleight of hand, an end in itself. Characteristic of the kind of response that *Flood* calls out is this observation
from a recent critic: "The title [*Flood*] is basically psychological in reference: the flood is that of memory and consciousness. It is also the
flood of modernism that threatens to obliterate the past, as the literal
TVA flooding will obliterate Fiddlersburg; more generally, as in the
poetry, it is the flood of Time and History; in the religious sense, it is
the Biblical flood that punished sin and gave the opportunity for a fresh
start, hence baptismal and redemptive drowning, death by water and
rebirth."[6] As this passage illustrates, part of the irritation of the book
is not only the unattractive character of its protagonist, but also a kind
of allusiveness run riot, a feeling that everything really means something else, a sense that ambiguity is an end in itself. Warren has, with
some justice, complained about the overreading of his novels, but his
tendency toward mechanical structuring and his penchant for allegorical names do nothing to discourage such readings.

The rhetorical inflation and artificiality of the style of *Flood* contribute to a more fundamental sense of falsity. The novel does not
engender the kind of imaginative sympathy which might be expected
from "a romance of our time." The reason lies in the brooding presence which hovers omnisciently over the action and comments, usually
sourly, on the characters. The point can perhaps best be illustrated by
the minor characters. The psychoanalyst Dr. Sutton may have tried to
help Lettice Poindexter, but the narrator reveals that the doctor's
repulsive bulk disguises a "hulking, wheezy" Indiana farm boy as troubled as his patients. The New York editor Telford Lott may have
staked his reputation on Bradwell Tolliver's early short stories and then
supported him through his later difficulties, but the narrator is not
fooled. Lott is a fraud. Then there is the young engineer Digby "with
his round face, freckles, perky red nose, sandy crew cut, grin exposing
square teeth with spaces too wide between them." The narrator
despises Digby for being . . . Digby. The aspirant actor Abbott Sprigg
has challenged New York and come trailing back to Fiddlersburg, but
his failure calls out not sympathy from the narrator but contempt. No
human frailty escapes. Even the French teacher in the Fiddlersburg
High School cannot hide his pathetic pretensions from the scathing
narrator. Only the black preacher, Leon Pinckney, and the Jewish tailor, Israel Goldfarb, get off scotfree, two types exempt from criticism
by the trendy liberalism of the early 1960s.

Although an enormous amount of technical skill and imaginative structuring have been lavished on *Flood*, it is, finally, an artificial, life-denying performance. Like *The Cave*, the novel ends on a note of affirmation, in the discovery by Bradwell Tolliver, italicized for the reader, that *"There is no country but the heart."* At the sight of a group of townspeople at the final prayer meeting as the waters rise, his eyes fill with tears. The scene is false, the gesture gratuitous. Bradwell Tolliver has violated his own theory of art and has failed to follow the logic of his story to its inevitable ending. The reader has long since begun to question the understanding of a character whose range of sympathy is so narrow and whose cynicism is so corrosive. The reader can scarcely be expected to sympathize with, or believe in, the new, sentimental Bradwell Tolliver who presumably has earned his redemption.

IV   Meet Me in the Green Glen

Although seven years separate *Flood* from Warren's next novel, *Meet Me in the Green Glen* (1971), the two books share a number of similarities. Both are set in the "Parkerton-Fiddlersburg Region" and the area they depict, by the conclusion of the action, has vanished, obliterated by the rising waters of an enormous reservoir. It exists only in the memories of a few souls either living on the shores of the lake or relocated by federal money.

The novels fill gaps in the history of that section of Tennessee which Warren has chosen for his own. William Faulkner toward the end of his career was conscious of rounding out the Yoknapatawpha Saga. Ellen Glasgow tells us in the prefaces to her collected works of the dawning realization that she had been writing a comprehensive social history of the South and of her subsequent resolution to complete it. Perhaps Warren has had a similar motive in continuing to explore the Parkerton-Fiddlersburg Region.

Although both novels are set in the period immediately before and after World War II, in tone and subject matter *Meet Me in the Green Glen* seems a return to a much earlier time. *Flood* is very much up to date with its references to New York and Hollywood, its concern with the politics of urban liberals, and its attentiveness to trends and fashions. *Meet Me in the Green Glen*, by contrast, has a remote, old-fashioned air and is often reminiscent in atmosphere of Faulkner, of turn-of-the-century stories like "That Evening Sun," or, for that matter, of Warren's own early stories in *The Circus in the Attic*.

The two epigraphs to the novel, taken from John Clare and Andrew

Marvell, announce that the theme is love and define the polarities
between which the novel turns. The stanza of the ballad by Clare
speaks with assurance of the promise of love romantically fulfilled. The
lines from Marvell describe a love tragically thwarted, "begotten by
Despair upon Impossibility."

The green glen of the novel is Spottwood Valley in Cardwell
County, Tennessee, a garden evoked by Warren with obvious nostalgia
and delight. The affectionate descriptions of the natural world are rendered with a precision and sensuousness now commonplace in his
poetry. Lyrical passages like the following abound:

The breeze had died down, but the air smelled sweet of rain coming. He
heard the musical rustle and stitch of the stream that spilled down from the
upper pasture along the rail fence of the yard and, farther down, yonder in
the darkness of the creek, where, before long now, the lake would be. Over
the valley, the sky was milky with mist. (375)

Warren has in this novel meticulously catalogued the artifacts of his
youth which are threatened by advancing technology: iron stoves,
crock jugs, slop jars, grindstones, plow-points. Before the wave of progress submerges them, Warren seems determined to record the precise
surfaces and textures of log house and tar-paper shanty, of general store
and county courtroom. The book is alive with the look and feel of
country things: killing a pig, dressing a rabbit, repairing a tractor. At
the conclusion a backwoodsman called Cy Grinder, won by his experience to some measure of content, hopes that he may have a "grandson to take with him to the woods, to teach quietness to and all the
sleights and knowledge he had grown into over the years, even if folks
out in the world never seem to care anymore" (340). *Meet Me in the
Green Glen* seems to have been written in part from an impulse not
unlike Cy Grinder's.

The opening chapter plunges the reader at once into two shocking
scenes of indiscriminate violence. A horse is ridden until, foaming and
wind-broken, it drops from exhaustion and then is senselessly slaughtered with a bullet behind the ear. Next a beautiful deer is shot with
a bow and arrow, a killing which at once provokes a quarrel between
former lovers. The ugliness of these actions and of the characters who
commit them stands in jarring contrast to the paradisaical green glen.

The activating circumstance of the novel resembles *Flood*. This
time, however, the character who disrupts the sleepy life of a rural

backwater is not a native son returning rich and famous but rather an illiterate Italian immigrant, Angelo Passetto, a swarthy ex-convict as unassimilable in xenophobic Spottwood Valley as a black man. "That Angelo fellow," one character says, "is not much more than a spit and holler from being a nigger himself" (251). Angelo Passetto unwittingly sets in motion a chain of circumstances that leads to his execution in Fiddlersburg penitentiary for the murder of a man he did not kill and with whom he could not even communicate.

The events of the narrative focus on the interrelations of three married couples. The couples represent familiar southern types, or perhaps, more accurately, familiar Warren types. Sunderland Spottwood of Spottwood Valley is masterful, coarse, well-born, and ornery. Late in life he takes as his second wife Cassie Killigrew, the woman toward whom all the men in the story are irresistibly drawn. Why this is so is as mysterious in the novel as it often is in life. Cassie's attraction is not passion, nor money, nor intelligence, nor charm, for she possesses none of these. She does exhibit in certain moods the kind of childlike vulnerability which might call out in one type of man the protective instinct that he might in turn mistake for love. But since her character is contradictory, and since she ends in madness, the reader must decide on her appeal largely on the testimony of the omniscient narrator. Many years younger than Sunderland Spottwood, she ends up nursing the inert hulk of his body, for his mind is destroyed by a massive stroke.

Cassie Killigrew and Sunderland Spottwood are supported in their dilapidated house by the secret philanthropy of Murray Guilfort. Guilfort is a homegrown carpetbagger: ruthless, booksmart, envious, and ambitious. In his restless, loveless search for meaning, he rises to the Tennessee Supreme Court, on the way marrying the plain but rich Bessie Darlington. Murray Guilfort gets to savor the satisfaction that Charles Lamb thought was the sweetest in life—to do a good deed in secret and have it found out by accident. He enjoys another satisfaction. He finds that his indiscretions with high-priced call girls in Chicago, also discovered by accident, do not destroy him professionally in Parkerton but make him a culture hero to streetcorner loungers and hasten his rise to the Supreme Court. But these satisfactions cannot fill the emptiness of his life, and he ends it with a drug overdose.

Against the blighted lives of Sunderland Spottwood and Murray Guilfort, both destroyed by their excesses, is set the life of Cy Grinder. The first lover of Cassie Killigrew but rejected as unworthy by her mother, Cy leads a life of violence and drift, then returns to the Valley

and coldly marries the grotesque Gladys Peegrum, and ends up as a
forester on the shores of the reservoir. The reader is assured that, in the
simplicity of his life in the green glen close to nature, he has found
some measure of happiness. Cassie Killigrew and Cy Grinder are yet
another example of Warren's fascination with lovers whose resolve not
to consummate their love is in part their undoing.

Cassie Killigrew is at the center of the story, a woman whose life
tied to an invalid has left her frustrated and unfulfilled. Already at
forty-two the victim of one nervous breakdown which hospitalized her
for four years, she senses the possibility of a new life with the unexpected coming of Angelo Passetto, a man eighteen years younger than
she. The white southern woman and the dark stranger embark in the
green glen on a bizarre affair. Carrie spies on him as he works about
the place. Sensing her interest, he coldly and mechanically rapes her:
"The spasm seemed impersonal in its automation, not involving him,
as though it were not even happening to him" (71). To sustain his
appetite for this unusually unattractive woman, he dresses her in black
lingerie and red satin and prepares for the periodic assault with the
contents of a bottle of whisky. The outcome of this improbable liaison
is Cassie Killigrew's remarkable announcement, "I love you—Angelo
Passetto."

Angelo abruptly begins a pursuit of Charlene, the mulatto daughter
of Sunderland Spottwood. Angelo first offends the folkways of Parkerton by declaring himself a black and trying to take Charlene to the
local movie house. When the lovers attempt to flee to the North, Cassie
first gives her blessing and her purse, then murders Sunderland in a
way designed to throw the blame on Angelo. He is tried, convicted,
and executed in a powerful sequence of scenes in which Warren's storytelling gifts are fully engaged. At the end Cassie Killigrew, like
Blanche DuBois in A Streetcar Named Desire, finds repose in insanity.

If the above summary sounds unconvincing, the novel is scarcely
more persuasive and the reason is not far to seek. Meet Me in the
Green Glen carries even further than Flood the Warren tendency to
become less interested in the people who populate his fiction than in
the ideas they represent. As he has become increasingly satisfied with
his philosophic formulations, his characters are not so much fallible
human beings imperfectly working out their destinies as abstractions
demonstrating a thesis. Not only has the style hardened into manner-
ism, but the ideas have lost their suppleness. What is missing is the
sense, so powerful in the earlier work, of testing ideas instrumentally.

Warren's meditations on Time, Change, Reality, and Selfhood are no longer integrated into the action. Rather, the reader repeatedly comes upon undigested and indigestible chunks of philosophic rhetoric of which the following is typical:

He began to create a Time of which the days would be a part, a Time in which things could exist and change, a Time that would stretch backward and forward and that you could think about. There were things you could do that would help make a picture of yourself in Time, and therefore make you real. (170)

There is the familiar if now largely unfelt nihilism which is insisted upon:

Why couldn't he [Murray Guilfort] be like Sunder, who had known nothing, who cared nothing, whose own image of Sunderland Spottwood was that of an angry, laughing self clamped astride a great beast that reared triumphantly against a world of nothingness, and who plunged ahead into the darkness of time, his eyes bulging bright and lips damp with the spittle from a last yell of manic glee? (34)

We are told again and again that things are "tied together" (63) and that the peculiarity of the South is its exaggerated sense of "loneliness" (334–45). The imagery, too, is reminiscent: the obsessive metaphors of flight, bleeding away, cave and womb, and rebirth. The constant editorializing is emphasized by the omniscient narrator who begins to sound like a backwoods evangelist. There are odd and disturbing shifts in tone. Angelo Passetto, brutish and inarticulate, suddenly thinks of "darkly glimmering opacity" (114). Finally all these characters begin to sound distressingly alike.

The reader of Warren feels that philosophically he is stacking the deck against his characters. The rigidity of his ideas is nowhere better illustrated than in the treatment of the theme of love in *Meet Me in the Green Glen* and in *Flood*. In a long fictional career, Warren has shown no willingness to deal with the most obvious product of love— children. What other author writing today has invented so many sexually active characters who have produced so few offspring? The emptiness of their existence, the sterility of their lives, the despair and loneliness that overwhelm these characters is seldom assuaged by the fundamental satisfaction of the gift of life. Many Warren characters might have less cause to whine if they sought some purpose outside themselves, if their compulsive search for "joy" could find some object beyond their own egos.

The lack of generations in Warren's fiction is the more surprising in that the family has been such an omnipresent force in southern society, surviving longer, or at least more conspicuously, in that region than in other sections of the country. The family still counts in the South. Nowhere is this more obvious than in the reverence for the family name, and familial loyalty is repeatedly recognized in the names southerners give their children. Warren's novels are imbued with this sense of family loyalty and dynasty. Edwina Parker lives in the old Parker Place on Parker Street in Parkerton. Sunderland Spottwood lives in Spottwood Valley. Calvin Fiddler returns to Fiddlersburg, the only place where his name does not sound funny.

Yet Warren's characters seldom have to face the most obvious consequence of their sexuality. Bradwell Tolliver does not want children, and when Lettice gets pregnant (accidentally), she has a convenient miscarriage. The birth of her child would have posed threatening problems to both the philosophy of the novel and its plot. Maggie Fiddler has no children. Only when safely on a Greek island and out of the picture is she allowed to get pregnant by Yasha Jones. When, late in *Meet Me in the Green Glen*, we have a long account of the lawyer Leroy Lancaster, we learn of him and his wife: "They never had a child" (272). Angelo Passetto rapes Cassie Killigrew. "Then one morning, the fifth morning, she had been there again, and he knew it had been her period. So everything was as it had been, and he did not know what he felt about that, either" (118). Warren characters seldom do know, or even pause to consider, how they might feel about "that." After Cassie Killigrew declares her love for Angelo Passetto, they set about raising not children but chickens.[7]

V   *Not So Much Created as Assembled*

The Cave, Flood, and *Meet Me in the Green Glen* are all remarkable books. Nobody writing today knows more about craftsmanship than Robert Penn Warren, and the effects he can produce are fresh and startling. In reading these novels, one can open to almost any page and find the arresting phrase and the telling observation which are his hallmark. But having said all this, the reader is likely to feel a sense of gifts squandered and opportunities lost. So many of these characters are predictable, for Warren seldom notes how often life casts against type. Liquor is more and more a cause and a resolution, and while that may be a faithful reflection of American life, it is not news and it is not, alas, very interesting. These novels seem at times only half-written, as if they were not so much created as assembled. The descriptions of the modern South carry neither the conviction nor the authority of the early novels, but seem often attenuated and remote. The preoccupation with the sexual life of the characters is often dull and occasionally funny, for, as Warren himself observes in his next novel, there is a concern with "the logistics, geometry and clinicism of the event."

The reader of fiction does not require that the ideas of a novel be "true," for most readers, at least the readers Warren might expect to attract, will have long since despaired of conclusively validating any philosophic scheme. What the reader requires of the philosophic novelist is that his ideas be dramatized, that the issues at stake be shadowed forth in the tension and conflict of human action. *All the King's Men* superbly fulfills this requirement. Jack Burden's ideological odyssey is not only provocative intellectually, but it is compelling emotionally. What Jack believes matters, matters to Jack and to the reader.

In these later novels, the characters too often stand for ideas rather than stand up for them. As a consequence, the reader may feel somewhat akin to a spectator at a performance of jugglers or gymnasts. He may be entertained by them, and even awed by their dexterity and their artistry, but he feels no identity with the performers nor does he feel any commitment to them. And only very rarely, and in very special cases, does fiction succeed without, in some degree, generating identity and commitment.

CHAPTER 8

Elder Statesman

A WRITER who lives to a great age in our Republic can expect to find himself an institution. The cult of the celebrity has given the artist a prominence he has seldom had before, and Robert Penn Warren has not escaped. The page "About the Author," which, since *Wilderness*, has been bound into each of his books, tells the lengthening story. Among the many honors bestowed upon him was an invitation in 1974 to give the third Jefferson Lecture in Washington, an occasion which produced his essay published the following year as *Democracy and Poetry* (1975).

I Democracy and Poetry

Such public occasions seem to require punditry under full sail with a heavy ballast of erudition. Warren did not disappoint. Taking for his theme the relation of American writers to the great experiment of democratic government in the New World, he retells the story of high-brow disenchantment with lowbrow money grubbing. The Founding Fathers envisioned a nation of free men. What they got were men enslaved to materialism who in their blind pursuit of prosperity hastened toward the annihilation of the self. As for our poetry, by which Warren intends all art, it is cast in the unenviable role of the bearer of evil tidings.

The tale has been more than twice-told, and Warren's version is a forceful reminder both of the widening gap between our aspirations and our history, and of the remarkable variety of artists who have swelled the chorus of doom-sayers.

Although offering itself as a reasoned critique of our national destiny, *Democracy and Poetry* is more a free-wheeling collection of aphorisms and capsule theories. Given the abstraction of the theme, not much more could be expected. The tone of the published text is mixed, the asides of platform delivery intermingled with passages of extreme philosophical density.

For the reader of Warren's poetry and fiction, the essay demonstrates how thoroughly elaborated is his concept of selfhood, a concept everywhere latent in the later fiction. In this slender volume Warren takes pains to make his view of the self explicit. His definition is indistinguishable from classical existentialism: "The self is never to be found, but must be created, not the happy accident of passivity, but the product of a thousand actions, large and small, conscious or unconscious, performed not 'away from it all,' but in the face of 'it all.' . . . The self is a style of being, continually expanding in a vital process that is the image, we may say, of the life process of a healthy society itself" (89).

II   A Place to Come To

At the end of the preface to *Democracy and Poetry,* Warren asks the question, "Who wants to be a superfluous man?" His next, and most recent, novel addresses itself to that question. The hero of *A Place to Come To* (1977), Jediah Tewksbury, is a representative man, the child of our time who rises in the world in a thoroughly modern way, that is, he manipulates the meritocracy. The educational system, the army, and the moneyed formless society of post–World War II offer him the means to rise from lowly origins to fame and fortune. Warren endows his hero with everything. Healthy and good-looking, Jed Tewksbury is an athletic star, a war hero, and a brilliant student. Worshiped by the young and adored by women, he is famous on two continents for his scholarship. His only child is a young genius at MIT. Jed is, moreover, free. What man could ask for more? Well, this is a Warren hero, and so he naturally asks what it all means and, as a consequence, frets himself into a severe case of worthlessness. He comes to feel that his existence has been a futile exercise in filling up time, that he is, in fact, a superfluous man.

Among Warren's novels *A Place to Come To* is unique in several ways. It is the only one of the ten in which the protagonist, in the great tradition of the novel, tells his own life story from birth to late middle age. Each of the other novels is limited in time. Three are historical— *World Enough and Time, Band of Angels,* and *Wilderness*—and of necessity evoke a lost world which can be recaptured only through imaginative reconstruction from documentary evidence. The remaining six novels span Warren's own life and follow one another in roughly chronological order. To recapitulate: *Night Rider* is the world of his boyhood; *At Heaven's Gate* is the Nashville of his college years; *All the King's Men* is the Louisiana he knew as a young teacher in Baton Rouge; the next three novels—*The Cave, Flood*, and *Meet Me in the Green Glen*—cover the years in his section of the South from just before World War II through the 1960s.

Warren has, in other words, been mining his own experience methodically, and the novels form not only a systematic record but a chronological sequence. In this sequence, *A Place to Come To* is the capstone. The central character, in a reflective mood which deepens as the book unfolds, looks back over a long career which is roughly contemporary with that of the author. Warren is clearly writing in a spirit of summary. Much of the novel, especially its closing section, has an elegiac tone. The hero is approaching old age and, if not content, is at least reconciled to his condition. The book's title is ambiguous: the place to come to is, ultimately, the grave; but the novel itself is the place that Jed Tewksbury has come to, the hero at the penultimate stage of his life journey.

Warren's novels are, as we have seen, unified in both locale and theme. They are books about the South and about southerners, and, while aspiring to transcend their time and place, they are nonetheless marked by a southern particularity which is deliberate, insistent, and unmistakable. When a character does leave home, as Bradwell Tolliver does in *Flood*, the novel gives us almost no sense of his distant environment or of his life in it. Abruptly breaking from this pattern, *A Place to Come To* follows its central character not only out of the South but out of the United States as well. Jed says he knows Chicago better than any place in the world, an observation impossible for any other Warren character to make. The freshness and power of the scenes in Chicago and Italy are sufficient to make the reader wish that Warren had emancipated his characters long ago. *A Place to Come To*, with its appealing breadth and amplitude, is Warren's most engaging fiction since *All the King's Men*.

Jed Tewksbury has a dramatic story to tell. He shares, it is true, the inability of Warren heroes to enter imaginatively into the lives of fulfilled people. For example, speaking of a couple farming outside of Nashville, Jed remarks: "There I began, too, to suffer envy at the simple completeness of their life, their obvious and unashamed satisfaction with each other, . . . their total absorption in the world of their creation. But, with some bitterness, I suppose, I would ask myself what their world meant: a charade of the past" (146). The observation is characteristic. Without much wrenching, it could be switched from novel to novel and from narrator to narrator. It sums up the typical Warren hero's tragic flaw—a failure of imaginative sympathy. Jed lacks it as well. Nor has he escaped the compulsion to define himself or the itch to weigh the meaning of everything, but he subordinates these traits to the narrative line, which is direct and compelling. He is the most likable of all Warren's heroes.

A Place to Come To is Warren's Horatio Alger novel, the rags-to-riches story of a "pore white trash" boy from the boondocks of Alabama who rises to be a great international scholar and academic celebrity. His rise is the more spectacular in that his origins are so humble, only sharecroppers and blacks occupying lower rungs on the social ladder of rural Alabama. The childhood he has to describe is a very American one: struggling through the Depression with fringe jobs, fame as a high-school athlete, sexual initiation, the trauma of the prom, the solution to one's problems by pulling up stakes. Grown to manhood, Jed confesses that he can neither remember nor feel a kinship with the child he was, a deficiency that the reader is likely to share. Jed's only link to his past seems to be a retentive memory for a sandhill cracker accent and a stock of folksy metaphors. So remote is he from the child he was that he occasionally slips over into the third person in describing this earlier self. Warren seems to have endowed Jed with such a past in something of the same spirit that Parson Weems had the young Washington cut down the cherry tree. Jed is a symbolic figure, and his childhood is mythic, the sort of childhood such a hero ought to have.

For Jed Tewksbury is the modern man, the existential man, the man both blessed and cursed with perfect freedom. Haunted by the outsized figure of his real father, Buck Tewksbury, Jed sees his life bracketed by two surrogate fathers: the elegant and accomplished Professor Stahlmann, "a profoundly kind man" who charts Jed's academic career, and the dim and ineffectual stepfather, Perk Simms, who offers an example of simple goodness and affection. Professor Stahlmann is the deracinated intellectual who resolves the emptiness of his life in the standard existential way—suicide. Perk Simms is everything Professor Stahlmann is not—illiterate, provincial, uncouth—but whatever his secret, and he has found the peace that passeth understanding, his stepson, Jed Tewksbury, has not the simplicity of heart to enter into it.

Jed's progress as an academic is only lightly sketched in the novel. It is the standard pattern of academic careerism, the bright young protégé who pledges himself to a sponsor and then rises, article by article and book by book, publishing and prospering. Like a number of his distinguished predecessors, Jed takes a kind of perverse pride in the fact that some of the literature he studies is of little intrinsic worth. He is a technician, takes pride in his technique, and comes to feel that the most he can hope for in his graduate students is that they become good technicians. He even envies the pure physicist whose work does not force him to a consideration of the human condition.

Although Jed is a professor, *A Place to Come To* is not an academic novel, and what gives shape to Jed Tewksbury's life is not the path of his teaching and research but his adventures with women and his quest for a spiritual father. In the opening scene of the novel, the boy's ne'er-do-well father plunges drunkenly from the front of his wagon while urinating on the hindquarters of a mule and is killed as the wheel rolls over his neck. That image haunts the hero throughout the novel. At crucial moments in his own development, when he senses that he has stumbled into a new world that is redefining him to suit itself, he retells the story in dialect as if to rebuff the seducers, reaffirm his old self, and resist the world that threatens to assimilate him. In each instance, whether at a graduate-school party or in the *beau monde* of Nashville, Tennessee, the consequences are the same and quite other than he anticipates: the auditors become convinced that he is a man of exceptional spiritual strength.

The special charm of Jed Tewksbury is easy enough to understand. First of all, it is not difficult to identify with success, and Jed's is a success story. He is, moreover, modest about his triumphs and generous in his judgments of others. Were we not persuaded by his own character, we have the testimony of all the women he meets. They all adore him.

Beginning with his mother, a creature of earth if ever there was one (her letters are the comic triumph of the novel), every woman he meets finds him irresistible. The queen of Dugton High School, Rozelle Hardcastle, invites him to the senior prom. And when he walks out, she spends her life trying to get him back. Once in graduate school, he enjoys the favors of the beautiful and voluptuous Dauphine Finkel in her elegant apartment over an old carriage house. Back from the war, he marries Agnes Andresen, the most eligible graduate student at the University of Chicago, so effortlessly taking her from her fiancé that Jed does not even know of his rival's existence.

Fleeing from Chicago to Nashville after Agnes's death, he is propositioned by an attractive woman drinking in the parlor car. When he rather brutally rejects her advances, she is charmed by his rudeness and writes him, enclosing a provocative picture. He is not interested.

Once he is established at Nashville, his circle conspires to match him with the most eligible single woman in the city, Maria McInnes. She too is perfect. "She had every virtue and every grace to be expected in the daughter of a rich Nashville banker of good family" (145). Maria naturally falls in love with Jed.

Giving Dante lessons to the aging but still immensely attractive Rebecca Jones-Talbot, he is led upstairs at the end of a lesson for a one-afternoon stand, no strings attached.

Later Jed will marry Dauphine Finkel, still rich and luscious, and, in addition, a famous photographer. She will bear his paragon of a son. He offers to go back to her at the end of the novel, and the reader no more doubts that Jed will get her back than the reader believes that her return will make Jed happy.

Along the way there are Roman women, "nigger gals," and at least one gorgeous graduate student.

These various conquests are related almost in passing. For the central action of the novel is a torrid love affair with Rozelle Hardcastle. Rozelle is in a variety of ways the counterpart of Jed Tewksbury. He is an only child whose mother wants him gone; she is an orphan raised unwillingly by an aunt. Without the ties of family they are free to work out their lives untrammeled by the usual claims and complications. Both are destined to shake the dust of Dugton, Alabama, from their feet and to rise by their special gifts. Jed is a football star; Rozelle is a prom queen. Jed rises by scholarship, patronage, and merit. Rozelle rises (this is before women's liberation) by two clever marriages. Having both arrived, they meet in Nashville and enter upon an affair in the best tradition of star-crossed lovers.

The bulk of the narrative traces the natural history of a love affair, defining the stages as they unfold. Jed and Rozelle pass from Stage I, *carpe diem*, through Stage II, *in contemptu mundi:*

But the world survives all contempt, even that of lovers. . . . And so we have Stage III, and even as the world returns, the lover recognizes more sharply than ever its lineaments. Repudiation, by its very nature, leads to definition. Furthermore, the conflict with the world, raised to a new level and intensity, leads to a conflict between lovers: i.e., Stage IV. Each lover, we may say, becomes a part of the world that the other confronts, and inevitably, as in all cases, the first conflict of wills between Rozelle and me concerned the relation to the world outside our closed orbit. (210)

Warren stresses the intense physicality of the relationship, and at the center of the novel is a description of sexual intercourse which is a tour de force of tonal variety—an admixture of engineering, gymnastics, hydraulics, and physiology—and about as sensuous as a blueprint. It is also very funny. But the tone is mixed, and the reader may begin to suspect that the humor is not intended.

The relationship is doomed, and Warren, returning to one of his favorite ideas, speculates on the consequence for lovers who fail to consummate their relationship when the opportunity first occurs: "For I was asking myself—or rather, knew myself full of the unphrased question—what everything would have been like now, if, long back, on a June night, to the muffled music of the Dugton High Senior Prom going on in the gym I had not merely given Rozelle the single ritual kiss she had so piteously, and calculatingly, asked for, but had clutched her to me, across the distance of Chrysler seat leather and the impediment of the gearshift, and all the as yet undivulged accidents of time" (293). That question has plagued a number of Warren heroes. But uncharacteristically, Jed adds, "But things were the way they were."

This note of fatalism, of life as a logic too obscure even for someone as curious and bright and philosophic as Jed, is the prevailing note of the novel. True, Warren brings out his favorite ideas and once more holds them up to the light. Consider this passage which occurs early in the novel:

I had never been west before, and it was a new kind of loneliness. This new kind, I decided, comes because the distance is fleeing away from you, bleeding away from you in all directions, and if you can't stop the process you'll be nothing left except a dry, transparent husk, like a cicada's, with the ferocious sunlight blazing through it. So people out there just huddle together like cattle before a storm, but the storm is not of the sky and the elements. Indeed, it is felt most dangerously on the stillest day when the visible fleeing horizon shivers in the brightness of distance. The storm is a purely metaphysical twister that sucks up the self and carries it away. No, I'll go back to the other metaphor, a constant slow bleeding away into the four quarters of distance. (93)

The motif is flight, flight westward into loneliness. Since Jack Burden first jumped into his car to drive to California, Warren has launched his characters on such symbolic journeys. The imagery of bleeding and bright distances is overly familiar. Inevitably, the imagery leads to a symbol of the self which is not, however, allowed to make its own point but is explicated by the narrator. And finally, the narrator, unable to choose between metaphors, gives the reader both.

The paragraph is vintage Warren.

But these familiar images and oft-discussed philosophical questions are not tackled with the old zeal and urgency. For Jed says, "Whatever illusions I had started out with I had lost. I had only the old wisdom we all struggle so hard to get and always find we already had: every man has to lead his own life and has little chance of knowing what it means, anyway" (356). Jed here comes close to what Warren, in *Homage to Theodore Dreiser*, seems to feel is Dreiser's view of "the ultimate wisdom"; it "is to be unillusioned, but to know, in a strange paradoxical doubleness, the necessity of illusion. . . . The final illusion that creates individuality—the self" (85).

At the end Jed Tewksbury, in a ritual of conclusion, returns to the sites of the great events of his life, one by one, but threatens to go again, this time with his son. *A Place to Come To* comes round finally to the prediction for our civilization which is held out in *Democracy and Poetry*. The speech is given to a sympathetic character in the novel, a close friend of Jed's and a brilliant physicist who has seen the worst that the twentieth century has to offer:

"As for me," he said, "I have no country that I can recognize as my own, and I am trying to learn to be happy in that condition." And he began to speak of a countryless world to come. "We are merely feeling the first pangs of modernity," he affirmed, "the death of the self which has become placeless. We are to become enormously efficient and emotional mechanisms, that will know—if 'know' is not too old-fashioned a word to use in this context—how to breed even more efficient and more emotionless mechanisms." (348)

III   *Recent Poetry*

If Jed Tewksbury is suffering from considerable diminution of energy at the conclusion of *A Place to Come To,* his creator shows no sign of it. In 1978 Warren brought out a new book of poems, *Now and Then, Poems 1976–1978,* a collection which won him his third Pulitzer Prize, his second for poetry. Two years later, in 1980, he followed this critical success with another volume, *Being Here, Poetry 1977–1980.*

In continuing to write verse into his seventies, Warren joins a very
select group of poets which includes Thomas Hardy and William But-
ler Yeats. Warren's work can stand comparison with those great predecessors, for what Allen Tate said a half-century ago is as true as ever:
Warren's work has "power."[1]

The poems collected in *Now and Then* illustrate with diagrammatic
exactness the dual nature of Warren's poetic impulse. He has always
tended to write poems stemming either from an abstract idea or from
a specific event grounded in experience. *Now and Then* mirrors the
old division. Section One, "Nostalgia," describes in anecdotes strongly
autobiographical in tone yet another return to his boyhood world; Section Two, "Speculative," probes philosophic questions, often in the language of abstraction.

Now and Then is not, however, divided against itself. What gives it
unity is the persona behind the collection, a clearly delineated character. The speaker is usually alone, hearing or overhearing human life
pulsing in the middle distance, but seldom participating in the action.
He is usually the poet in a landscape—on a rocky height, in the forest,
by the seashore. The poems are haunted with images of sunset,
autumn, and death, and the collection has about it a quality of vale-
diction. Reality is often less substantial than dream. Four lines from
"Rather Like a Dream" are characteristic:

> I walk in the mountain woods,
> Alone, hour sunset, season
> When the first maple leaf falls red, the first
> Beech leaf gold. . . .

The speaker may be lying late in bed or dozing before a log fire.
Although not religious in any orthodox sense, he often finds occasion
to refer to or call upon God. The future plays little part in these poems,
the speaker preferring to cast his mind back over his own past and the
long reach of the human past.

The sensibility of the persona is one source of unity in these poems;
a second is the meditation on time: *then*—rural Kentucky and Tennessee in the early years of the century; *now*—an aging poet reflecting
on the meaning of his life. A youngster attends a revival meeting, speculates at night in the town cemetery, watches an orphanage boy kill a
critically ill bulldog and then burst into tears. In other poems the

speaker, now an old man ("sixty years blown like a hurricane past"), has returned. He either seeks out the friends of his youth or comes upon them in the streets of his hometown. Rich in reminiscence, these poems are written in the modulated and assured voice of a master craftsman.

The centerpiece of *Now and Then* is "Red Tail Hawk and Pyre of Youth." With a miraculous shot, the young hunter brings down a hawk which, transformed by the amateur taxidermist's art, stands for years above the favorite books of the by now quite literary young man. Considerably older and chastened by experience, the speaker finds the stuffed bird in an old lumber room and ritualistically destroys it by fire. Speculating on the persistence of the memory, the speaker feels that the rifle shot has in some mystic way bound him to the natural world:

> The old .30–30 that knows
> How to bind us in air-blood and earth-blood together
> In our commensurate fate,
> Whose name is a name beyond joy.

The poem is both a celebration of youthful innocence and a parable of the artist who in his making must destroy. The speaker, a modern-day Audubon, has slaughtered the bird to create the work of art—to fix it out of time. But he is troubled by the feeling of violation that has accompanied the act. Warren has said, "I am a yearner,"[2] and the speaker of this poem yearns to blend earth and air—flesh and spirit—if only in his last conscious moment of life.

The most recent volume of verse, *Being Here, Poetry 1977–1980*, testifies both to Warren's continuing creativity and to his tendency to fall into self-imitation. When a writer has written so much over so long a period of time, repetition is probably inevitable. "Safe in Shade," a boy listening to his Confederate grandfather, has been told before by Warren in poetry ("Court-Martial"), in prose ("When the Light Gets Green"), and in an essay ("Jefferson Davis Gets His Citzenship Back"). In "Night Watching," the poet watches his son lift his arms inexplicably toward the sky as he did in the earlier "Youth Stares at Minoan Sunset." The poet's puzzlement and wonder before "Truth" and "Time" are by now overly familiar as are a number of their metaphorical equivalents.

Being Here loosely collects fifty poems into what Warren calls, in an afterword, "a shadowy narrative, a shadowy autobiography." Arranged into five sections, the poems begin with boyhood and move through youth, young manhood, and maturity to old age. Warren is, as usual, concerned that the volume have a unity of its own. In the "Afterthought" he attempts to head off objections to his scheme by rationalizing several poems which look "rather like sore thumbs." But most readers will probably simply pick their favorites. Certainly "October Picnic Long Ago" and "Boyhood in Tobacco Country" represent Warren at the top of his form. Like Thomas Hardy, whom he resembles in a number of ways, Warren has written his most appealing lyrics from memories of early happiness with their poignant overtones of regret and loss.

The poems in both *Now and Then* and *Being Here* confront the same problems that have concerned Warren for a lifetime: the nature of time, the quest for and impossibility of perfect knowledge, the urgency of definition. They reveal the same restless inventiveness of language, particularly striking compounds, and unexpected ellipses and shifts in word order. The diction is occasionally tortured and convolved, descending at times into a kind of telegraphese. The rhythms vary from slack and roughened lines to, quite unexpectedly, a number of poems in rhymed stanzas. Lyricism has never been a Warren hallmark, and there is scarcely a poem that would lend itself to a musical setting.

Poetry is preeminently an affirmative art, yet many of these poems end with a question. Warren's tentativeness, increasingly evident in later years, has by now been erected into a principle: "I was forced," he said, "to think more and more about what survives imperfect techniques. An intuition somehow survives groping formulation, the imperfect formulation of it. And sometimes the imperfection of the formulation actually gives a peculiar poignance to the formulation."[3]

IV *Summing Up: A Romantic Genius*

Now and Then and *Being Here* are Warren's twelfth and thirteenth books of poetry. In addition, there have been, to date, ten novels, a volume of short stories, a play, a collection of critical essays, a biography, three historical essays, and two studies of race relations in America. To these must be added the textbooks and the fugitive pieces that remain uncollected.

Such productivity is extraordinary. As Eric Bentley once observed, Warren very nearly fulfills our idea of the romantic genius.[4] There is about his art the prodigality of the writer who exercises his verbal gifts for the sheer magic of the effects he can produce. Warren's language is robust and rhetorical. He likes his adjectives and nouns to go in pairs, reinforcing one another, begetting rhythm and resonance. When a comparison catches his fancy, his first metaphor is likely to suggest another, and he piles image on image as he warms to his task. As a result, he is led by his own ingenuity into the excesses of language which mar many otherwise fine passages. About all of Warren's work there is a gusto and masculine force, a willingness to risk bathos and absurdity, reminiscent of the writer who, Warren has said, has had the greatest influence on his own work—Shakespeare.

But despite the amount and variety of his work, Warren has held himself to a consistently high level of craftsmanship. From the beginning of his career, his analytical power and creative force have been disciplined by his critical intelligence and tempered by his formidable erudition. Warren's concern with literature is fundamental and inclusive. His discussions of other writers reveal this deeply serious commitment, for his criticism is warm in its enthusiasm and generous in its judgments, neither excessively formal nor overly intellectual.

One of the advantages of surveying all of Warren's writing is the awareness it gives us of his continuing vitality. His latest work testifies to his desire to find new solutions to artistic problems, and he will undoubtedly continue to seek for the meaning of his life and time. He has always seemed driven to explore the boundaries of his art, to try to push the possibilities of his form to its outer limits. Warren has said on more than one occasion that writing is a process of exploration, a means of probing and testing in which the artist discovers his meanings and, in defining them, defines himself. In 1957 he told Ralph Ellison: "All writing that is any good is experimental; that is, it's a way of seeing what is possible—what poem, what novel is possible. . . . You put the question to human nature—and especially your own nature—and see what comes out. It is unpredictable."[5] The freshness and energy of *A Place to Come To, Now and Then,* and *Being Here* suggest that it would be rash to predict what Warren will do next.

One of the best poems Warren has ever written, "American Portrait: Old Style," he placed first in *Now and Then.* The poet has sought out a trench in the woods where, as a boy sixty years before, he had in imagination wrestled the Shawnee or bayoneted the Yankee. On an impulse, he lies down in the trench and, staring up at the sky, wonders what it would be like to know himself dead. The voice of the closing stanza—reflective, affirmative, humane—is unmistakably the voice of Robert Penn Warren:

> But why should I lie here longer?
> I am not dead yet, though in years,
> And the world's way is yet long to go.
> And I love the world even in my anger,
> And love is a hard thing to outgrow.

Notes and References

Chapter One

1. *New York Herald Tribune Book Review*, October 11, 1953; see also Robert Penn Warren, "Jefferson Davis Gets His Citizenship Back," *New Yorker*, February 25, 1980, pp. 44–48.

2. Unless otherwise noted, page references to the works of Robert Penn Warren are to the first edition, cited in the bibliography.

3. Marshall Walker, *Robert Penn Warren: A Vision Earned* (Edinburgh, 1979), p. 250.

4. *Writers at Work*, ed. Malcolm Cowley (New York: Viking, 1959), pp. 186–87.

5. Donald Davidson, *Southern Writers in the Modern World* (Athens, Georgia, 1958), p. 16.

6. *Robert Penn Warren Talking: Interviews 1950–1978* (New York: Random House, 1980), p. 226.

7. *Fugitives' Reunion: Conversations at Vanderbilt*, ed. Rob Roy Purdy (Nashville: Vanderbilt University Press, 1959), pp. 116–17.

8. Allen Tate, "*The Fugitive* 1922–1925: A Personal Recollection Twenty Years After," *Princeton University Library Chronicle* 3 (April 1942): 81–82.

9. Louise Cowan, *The Fugitive Group: A Literary History* (Baton Rouge, 1959), p. 150.

10. Tate, p. 82.

11. *Fugitives' Reunion*, p. 119.

12. *Robert Penn Warren Talking*, p. 244.

13. Robert Penn Warren, *Who Speaks for the Negro?* (New York, 1965), p. 320.

14. *Fugitives' Reunion*, p. 209.

15. *Writers at Work*, pp. 191, 194.

16. Twelve Southerners, *I'll Take My Stand* (New York: Harper & Brothers, 1930), p. 59.

17. *Writers at Work*, p. 194.

18. *Fugitives' Reunion*, p. 210.

19. *Robert Penn Warren Talking*, p. 266.

20. "Robert Penn Warren," *Wilson Library Bulletin* 13 (June 1939): 652.

21. Harvey Breit, *The Writer Observed* (Cleveland: World Publishing Company, 1956), pp. 132–33. Interview of June 25, 1950.

22. *An Anthology of Stories from the Southern Review*, eds. Cleanth Brooks and Robert Penn Warren (Baton Rouge: Louisiana State University Press, 1953), p. xiii.

23. *Selected Essays* (New York, 1958), p. xi.

Chapter Two

1. Robert Lowell, "John Ransom's Conversation," *Sewanee Review* 56 (Summer 1948): 388.

2. John Crowe Ransom, "The Teaching of Poetry," *Kenyon Review* 1 (Winter 1939): 82.

3. Marshall Walker, *Robert Penn Warren: A Vision Earned*, p. 54.

4. Ibid., p. 58.

5. "The Themes of Robert Frost," *Selected Essays*, p. 125.

6. "Robert Penn Warren Reads from His Own Works," *Yale Series of Recorded Poets*, Carillon Records, New Haven, Connecticut.

7. "A Note on Three Southern Poets," *Poetry: A Magazine of Verse* 40 (May 1932): 110.

8. *Modern Poetry: American and British*, eds. Kimon Friar and John Malcolm Brinnin (New York: Appleton-Century-Crofts, 1951), pp. 542–43.

9. Ibid.

10. "The Themes of Robert Frost," p. 120.

Chapter Three

1. *Writers at Work*, p. 191.

2. Ibid.

3. These stories were collected in *The Circus in the Attic* (New York, 1948).

4. *Selected Essays* (New York, 1958), pp. 178–79.

5. *Writers at Work* p. 191.

6. *Robert Penn Warren Talking: Interviews 1950–1978*, p. 251.

7. Malcolm Cowley, "Luke Lee's Empire," *New Republic*, August 23, 1943, p. 258.

8. "Introduction," *All the King's Men* (New York, 1953), p. iii.

9. *Robert Penn Warren Talking*, pp. 108–109.

10. *Writers at Work*, p. 190.

11. *Selected Essays*, p. 81.

12. "William Faulkner," *Selected Essays*, pp. 59–79.

13. "T. S. Stribling: A Paragraph in the History of Critical Realism," *American Review* 2 (February 1934): 463–64.

14. "An American Tragedy," *Yale Review* 52 (Autumn 1962): 3.

15. "Introduction," *All the King's Men*, p. iv.

16. Edmund Wilson, *Axel's Castle* (New York: Charles Scribner's Sons, 1931), p. 25.

Chapter Four

1. *Fugitives' Reunion*, p. 208.

2. "Introduction," *All the King's Men*, pp. i–ii.

3. Ibid., p. iii.

4. *The Writer Observed*, p. 132.

5. Isabel Leighton, ed., *The Aspirin Age* (New York: Simon and Schuster, 1949), p. 339.

6. George E. Sokolsky, "Huey Long," *Atlantic Monthly* 156 (November 1935): 526.

7. Hartnett T. Kane, *Louisiana Hayride* (New York: Morrow, 1941), p. 225.

8. "Introduction," *Stories from the Southern Review*, eds. Cleanth Brooks and Robert Penn Warren (Baton Rouge: Louisiana State University Press, 1953), xiii.

9. "Introduction," *All the King's Men*, p. v.

10. Ibid., p. vi.

11. Ibid., p. iv.

12. Ibid., p. vi.

13. Ibid., p. ii.

14. See "Love and Separateness in Eudora Welty," *Selected Essays*, pp. 159–69.

15. See William M. Schutte, "The Dramatic Versions of the Willie Stark Story," *All the King's Men: A Symposium* (Pittsburgh: Carnegie Institute of Technology, 1957), pp. 75–90.

16. Wolcott Gibbs, *New Yorker*, January 24, 1948, p. 45.

17. *Selected Essays*, p. 57.

18. Ibid., p. 222.

19. Ibid., p. 228.

20. "Writer at Work: How a Story Was Born and How, Bit by Bit, It Grew," *New York Times Book Review*, March 1, 1959, p. 5.

21. Ibid.

Chapter Five

1. *Selected Essays*, p. 48.

2. *Writers at Work*, p. 196.

3. *Selected Essays*, p. 55.

4. "About the Author," *Saturday Review of Literature*, June 24, 1950, p. 11.

5. *Selected Essays*, p. 39.

6. Ibid., p. 54.

7. "The Way It Was Written," *New York Times Book Review*, August 23, 1953, p. 6.

8. Ibid.

9. *Writers at Work*, p. 189.

10. "The Way It Was Written," p. 6.

11. Ibid.

12. In 1979 Warren brought out a revised text of *Brother to Dragons, A Tale in Verse and Voices: A New Version*. A number of factors seem to have entered into Warren's decision to rewrite the original. Through a misunderstanding between author and editor, the 1953 text had been faulty. Also, Warren over the years had worked to prepare an acting version, and in 1964 *Brother to Dragons* was put on at the American Place Theater in New York City with subsequent productions in Providence and in Boston. Then, in 1977, Boynton Merrill, Jr., published a scholarly account of the general subject, *Jefferson's Nephews* (Princeton: Princeton University Press), which in part challenged Warren's version of the facts.

The preface to the new version is puzzling. While observing that the factual accuracy of the poem is not crucial to its success as a work of art, Warren is nevertheless rather defensive about his historical research. He points out that recent investigations, while correcting him on minor points, do not alter the basic thematic or dramatic outline. This defense of his use of evidence has at best only antiquarian interest and seems trivial in comparison to, say, the liberties he takes with the character of Thomas Jefferson. The controversy detracts from what really matters—the poem.

Equally puzzling is Warren's decision not to recast the work for the stage. "It is definitely not a play," he states in the preface, "and must not be taken as such." Yet the changes in the text—the cuts and the pacing—are obviously in the direction of greater actability. At the same time, some of the nuance and novelty of the first version are lost. Readers who have lived with the original text for seventeen years may reasonably wonder why Warren chose to expend his creative energy on another version of a closet drama.

13. *The Legacy of the Civil War* (New York, 1961), p. 50.

14. Leonard Casper, *Robert Penn Warren: The Dark and Bloody Ground* (Seattle, 1960), p. 188.

15. *Robert Penn Warren Talking: Interviews 1950–1978*, p. 253.

16. *Writers at Work*, p. 188.

17. Walker, *Robert Penn Warren: A Vision Earned*, p. 257.

18. *The Legacy of the Civil War*, p. 50.

19. Walker, *Robert Penn Warren*, p. 254.

20. *The Legacy of the Civil War*, pp. 83–84.

Chapter Six

1. *Robert Penn Warren Talking*, p. 120.
2. *Selected Essays*, p. 186.
3. "Writer at Work: How a Story Was Born and How, Bit by Bit, It Grew," *New York Times Book Review*, March 1, 1959, p. 5.
4. *Poet's Choice*, eds. Paul Engle and Joseph Langland (New York: Dial Press, 1962), p. 80.
5. *Selected Poems: New and Old, 1923–1966* (New York, 1966), p. vii.
6. Louise Cowan, *The Fugitive Group: A Literary History* (Baton Rouge, 1959), p. 150. Sidney Hirsch was one of the founders of the Fugitive group.
7. *Democracy and Poetry* (Cambridge, 1975), p. 74.
8. *Selected Poems of Herman Melville* (New York: Random House, 1970), p. 27.
9. *Robert Penn Warren Talking*, p. 110.
10. *John Greenleaf Whittier* (Minneapolis: University of Minnesota Press, 1971), p. 58.
11. *Poet's Choice*, p. 80.

Chapter Seven

1. *Robert Penn Warren Talking*, p. 136.
2. A. Walton Litz, "Literary Criticism," *Harvard Guide to Contemporary American Writing* (Cambridge: Harvard University Press, 1979), p. 56.
3. Frederick Lewis Allen, *Only Yesterday* (New York: Harpers, 1931), pp. 193–97.
4. *Newsweek*, May 4, 1964, p. 93; *Time*, April 24, 1964, p. 106; *New Yorker*, September 12, 1964, p. 40.
5. *Homage to Theodore Dreiser* (New York, 1971), p. 92.
6. Monroe K. Spears, *Dionysus and the City* (New York: Oxford University Press, 1970), p. 183.
7. *Brother to Dragons: A New Version* offers unexpected confirmation of this tendency. In discussing his use of historical evidence, Warren observes in passing: "I have disposed of a raft of young children as irrelevant to my theme" (p. xi).

Chapter Eight

1. Louise Cowan, *The Fugitive Group: A Literary History*, p. 150.
2. *Robert Penn Warren Talking*, p. 234.
3. Ibid., p. 166.
4. Eric Bentley, "The Meaning of Robert Penn Warren's Novels," *Forms of Modern Fiction* (Bloomington: Indiana University Press, 1948), p. 271.
5. *Writers at Work*, p. 198.

Selected Bibliography

PRIMARY SOURCES

Only separate books are listed. See Mary Nance Huff, *Robert Penn Warren: A Bibliography* (New York: David Lewis, 1968). A work sponsored by the American Bibliographical Society is in preparation.

1. Biography
John Brown: The Making of a Martyr. New York: Payson and Clarke, 1929.

2. Children's Books
The Gods of Mount Olympus. New York: Random House, 1959.
Remember the Alamo! New York: Random House, 1958.

3. Essays
Democracy and Poetry. Cambridge, Massachusetts: Harvard University Press, 1975.
Homage to Theodore Dreiser on the Centennial of His Birth. New York: Random House, 1971.
John Greenleaf Whittier. Minneapolis: University of Minnesota Press, 1970.
The Legacy of the Civil War: Meditations on the Centennial. New York: Random House, 1961.
Segregation: The Inner Conflict in the South. New York: Random House, 1956.
Selected Essays. New York: Random House, 1958.
Selected Poems of Herman Melville. New York: Random House, 1971.
Who Speaks for the Negro? New York: Random House, 1965.

4. Fiction
All the King's Men. New York: Harcourt, Brace and Company, 1946; Modern Library edition with introduction by the author, 1953.
At Heaven's Gate. New York: Harcourt, Brace and Company, 1943; reissued by Random House, 1959.
Band of Angels. New York: Random House, 1955.

The Cave. New York: Random House, 1959.

The Circus in the Attic and Other Stories. New York: Harcourt, Brace and Company, 1948.

Flood: A Romance of Our Time. New York: Random House, 1964.

Meet Me in the Green Glen. New York: Random House, 1971.

Night Rider. Boston: Houghton Mifflin and Company, 1939; reissued by Random House, 1948.

A Place to Come To. New York: Random House, 1976.

Wilderness: A Tale of the Civil War. New York: Random House, 1961.

World Enough and Time: A Romantic Novel. New York: Random House, 1950.

5. Play

All the King's Men: A Play. New York: Random House, 1960.

6. Poetry

Audubon: A Vision. New York: Random House, 1971.

Being Here. New York: Random House, 1980.

Brother to Dragons: A Tale in Verse and Voices. New York: Random House, 1953. Substantially revised and reissued in 1979 by Random House as *Brother to Dragons: A Tale in Verse and Voices: A New Version.*

Eleven Poems on the Same Theme. Norfolk, Connecticut: New Directions, 1942.

Incarnations: Poems, 1966–1968. New York: Random House, 1968.

Now and Then: Poems, 1976–1978. New York: Random House, 1978

Or Else—Poem/Poems 1968–1974. New York: Random House, 1974.

Promises: Poems 1954–1956. New York: Random House, 1957.

Selected Poems, 1923–1943. New York: Harcourt, Brace and Company, 1944.

Selected Poems, New and Old, 1923–1966. New York: Random House, 1966.

Selected Poems: 1923–1975. New York: Random House, 1976.

Thirty-Six Poems. New York: Alcestis Press, 1935.

You, Emperors, and Others: Poems 1957–1960. New York: Random House, 1960.

SECONDARY SOURCES

Only separate books can be mentioned. For a detailed list of American criticism consult Neil Nakadate, *Robert Penn Warren: A Reference Guide* (Boston: G. K. Hall & Co., 1977). See also the indexes to the annual volumes of *American Literary Scholarship*, published since 1963 by the Duke University Press.

BRADBURY, JOHN M. *The Fugitives: A Critical Account*. Chapel Hill: University of North Carolina Press, 1958. Useful chapters on Warren's poetry and fiction through 1956.

BROOKS, CLEANTH. *The Hidden God: Studies in Hemingway, Faulkner, Yeats, Eliot, and Warren*. New Haven: Yale University Press, 1963. Short account of Warren's characteristic themes with special attention to the Christian elements in his writing.

———. *Modern Poetry and the Tradition*. Chapel Hill: University of North Carolina Press, 1939. A helpful discussion of the early poetry.

CASPER, LEONARD. *Robert Penn Warren: The Dark and Bloody Ground*. Seattle: University of Washington Press, 1960. The first book-length study of Warren's work.

COWAN, LOUISE. *The Fugitive Group: A Literary History*. Baton Rouge: Louisiana State University Press, 1959. An account of Warren's relations with the Fugitives.

DAVIDSON, DONALD. *Southern Writers in the Modern World*. Athens: University of Georgia Press, 1958. Useful for its reminiscences of Warren as a student at Vanderbilt and his connection with the Fugitives.

GUTTENBERG, BARNETT. *Web of Being: The Novels of Robert Penn Warren*. Nashville: Vanderbilt University Press, 1975. A reading of the novels through *Meet Me in the Green Glen* with emphasis on the existential element.

LONGLEY, JOHN LEWIS, JR., ed. *Robert Penn Warren: A Collection of Critical Essays*. New York: New York University Press, 1965. Sixteen essays of varying merit on various topics.

STEWART, JOHN L. *The Burden of Time: The Fugitives and the Agrarians*. Princeton: Princeton University Press, 1965. Warren's career through the early 1960s in the context of the Fugitive movement.

STRANDBERG, VICTOR H. *The Poetic Vision of Robert Penn Warren*. Lexington: University of Kentucky Press, 1977. A thorough and stimulating discussion of the poetry; supersedes his *A Colder Fire* (1965).

WALKER, MARSHALL. *Robert Penn Warren: A Vision Earned*. Edinburgh: Paul Harris, 1979. A comprehensive discussion of Warren through *A Place to Come To;* includes a valuable interview with Warren in September 1969.

WEST, PAUL. *Robert Penn Warren*. Minneapolis: University of Minnesota Press, 1964. A short, impressionistic survey of Warren's work through *Flood*.

Index